Contents

Amy Amy Amy

The Amy Winehouse Story

by Nick Johnstone

OMNIBUS PRESS

London • Los Angeles • New York • Paris • Sydney • Copenhagen • Berlin • Madrid • Tokyo

Exclusive Distributors
Music Sales Limited,
14/15 Berners Street,
London, W1T 3LJ.

Music Sales Corporation,
257 Park Avenue South,
New York, NY 10010, USA.

Macmillan Distribution Services,
53 Park West Drive,
Derrimut, Vic 3030,
Australia.

Typeset by Phoenix Photosetting, Chatham, Kent
Printed in the EU

A catalogue record for this book is available from the British Library.

Visit Omnibus Press on the web at www.omnibuspress.com

Author's Note

Amy Winehouse was invited to participate in this telling of her story but did not reply, making this an unauthorised account of her career and life to date. Interviews were also requested with Darcus Beese, Raye Cosbert, Nick Godwin and Nick Shymansky, all of whom also declined or did not reply. I would therefore like to thank those who did agree to be interviewed and the many who offered help with research or volunteered information or detail.

Introduction To 2011 Edition

It was December 2007 and the photograph was shocking, as so many of the photographs of Amy Winehouse since have been shocking. This one, apparently taken at 5:40 am on Sunday, December 2, outside a residence in Bow, east London, depicted Amy in the street. Days earlier, in a media storm, she had walked out of her UK tour after a performance in Brighton. The rest of the dates were cancelled, seemingly on a doctor's orders. In the dark and freezing cold, there was Amy standing barefoot, wearing nothing but a pair of jeans and a red bra. The Ronnie Spector inspired beehive she had sported up to that point, in support of the already massively successful *Back To Black* album, had collapsed, and in its place her hair was long, flowing and natural. Over her heart, there was a tattoo that read 'Blake's pocket', Blake being Blake Fielder-Civil, her then husband, incarcerated, awaiting trial, at the time this photograph was taken. To the right of her exposed navel, a tattoo of an anchor, topped and tailed with the cliché: Hello Sailor. It was a reminder that the woman in the photograph, whose face, scrunched with pain and emotional suffering, as it was in so many pictures, still had a mischievous sense of humour. Tangled in the strap of her red bra, a crucifix (a curio for a Jewish girl) could be seen hanging from a rosary bead necklace, the kind you find either in Catholic gift shops or, back at that time, on sale at Top Shop on Oxford Street. Her feet were bare on the icy cold ground and her toes were painted red. Her underwear – black, with a white polka dot pattern – was peaking over the waist of her jeans.

In a year when photographs of Amy Winehouse in many states and shapes and guises and images dominated the media, each new picture surpassed the last, as she appeared to incrementally crumble under the cocktail that was the magnitude of her success, the constant media attention, her rocky relationship with Blake and her dangerously fast rock'n'roll lifestyle. Each image offered its clue to what had become a guessing game for millions, a guessing game which hinged – and kept hinging until July 23, 2011 – on one central question: what is wrong with Amy Winehouse?

Consider the facts at the time of this photograph that seems now like a prophecy of doom, the moment in the Amy Winehouse story when she crossed over from being a strong, opinionated maverick to being tragic: here was a supremely talented singer, songwriter, musician and performer, age 24, sitting at that young age at the top of the pile. In the precarious, transient world of pop music, she ended 2007 as arguably the most important and potent artist in the music business. And yet behind the accolades, look at that year's drama: erratic performances, tours cancelled before they even started or midway through, drunken TV appearances, a drug overdose, her parents giving candid mum'n'dad interviews, a whirlwind marriage to a husband who ended the year behind bars charged with attempting to pervert the course of justice, her in-laws giving interviews, rumours of self harm, depression and bulimia, those photos of her blood stained ballet pumps the night of the bust-up with Blake at the Sanderson Hotel in Central London, writing 'I Love Blake' across her stomach with a shard of broken mirror during a photoshoot with *Spin* magazine, the will-she-won't-she dance with the tabloids regarding speculation over whether *Back To Black*'s storming lead single 'Rehab' would end up proving painfully prophetic (and how it did).

The drama was the music and the music was the drama. Her turbulent, heart-on-sleeve lifestyle made the music what it was: she wrote about her life, what happened to her. And this proved irresistible to fans and media alike: a woman whose rawness, whose vulnerability, was the same on and off record. Somewhere along the way, in the massive success of *Back To Black*, Amy Winehouse the person became more famous than Amy Winehouse the singer; she gave the gossip columnists a ready-to-go soap opera, the kind of which hadn't been seen since Kurt Cobain exploded onto the mainstream psyche with Nirvana's *Nevermind* and then exploded just as quickly out of it, the fatal day he shot himself. In the end, it seemed she got lost in her own myth, too.

Her voice was astonishing. It could throw goose bumps up your arms. Few who heard it before knowing much about the singer heard the voice of a white singer. Most, myself included, assumed it was the voice of a black American singer. Jazzy, bluesy, with some contemporary R&B and hip hop leanings – someone like Erykah Badu or Alicia Keys, for instance. That the singer turned out to be a petite white Jewish North London woman stunned even the most seasoned ears, the most passionate of music lovers. How was it possible that someone that young was able to communicate such life lived? Of course, she was the real thing, that's why – an artist, with all the inner conflict and turbulence that goes with the terrain. Billie Holiday had it. Elvis Presley had it. Joe Strummer had it. Kurt Cobain had it. James Brown had it. Bob Dylan has it, Keith Richards has it, Lou Reed has it. And for sure, Amy Winehouse had it. Why else such terrible lows inspiring such magical music? Why else the fallow periods in her songwriting followed by hyperproductive brilliance riding the dark loop of a personal crisis? Why else all the relentless drinking and smoking and drug abuse? How else to explain the drastic change in her personal appearance and body image between her debut album *Frank* in October 2003 and *Back To Black* in October 2006? How else to explain the hit and miss live performances? One show stuns the audience with its exuberance and irreverence and passion and the next stuns the audience with its shapelessness, its lack of centre, its fundamental absence of fire and Amy's inability to lock in with her band, with the songs, with the moment, or even remember the words. How else to explain a song like 'Rehab', which issues a feelgood Sixties retro pop blast while discussing what for many is a matter of life and death, and what became for Amy quite literally a matter of life and death.

That song, in its tease, was probably what set the fatal ending in motion: in dishing a celebrity obsessed media a provocative and not entirely unplayful song like 'Rehab', she invited a fascination with her private life, one that soon spiralled hideously out of control and became a day by day pursuit of her most private truth. The cameras and reporters asked endlessly: is she really doing cocaine and heroin and crack? Is she really self harming? Is she really a depressive? Is she happy to be this successful? Is she miserable being this successful? Do she and Blake really want to move to Miami and have lots of kids? Is she really a woman still crushed by her parents separating when she was nine? Will she walk out on her music at some point? Will her fans keep tolerating all the no shows and cancellations or will they eventually feel let down one too many times and switch their adoration elsewhere? Will she go into rehab in the end or has she got her life under control despite the stories we read in the tabloids day in, day out?

Eventually, as had happened to Kurt Cobain, she seemed trapped by the fame, wanting only to return to the simplicity of making music. She started learning the drums, perhaps to try to regain that purity of music and in what is believed to have been her last interview, with the *The Daily Telegraph*, in March 2011, she talked of a hope to study music, "I would love to study guitar or trumpet. I can play a lot of different instruments adequately but nothing really well. If you play an instrument, it makes you a better singer. The more you play, the better you sing, the more you sing, the better you play." But that plan never was to materialize. Her death happened suddenly and even though the threat of it had been circling her for what felt like ages, it was still utterly shocking.

Not so long before, she was just a girl who grew up in love with music, a love of music handed to her by her family. When she discovered her talent – that voice, the songwriting ability, the knack for writing deceptively simple lyrics which resonated – she moved fast and things moved fast and suddenly she was bigger than she must have ever imagined being. But then she got stuck. And the door she'd opened welcomed in a host of British female artists inspired by her, like Adele and Duffy. The omnipresent anticipation of a third album, rumoured to have been underway since early 2008, kept everybody waiting with baited breath. Then, just when it seemed she had turned a corner, was turning a corner, when there might be another raw, candid, remarkable album on her record label's schedule, came the tragic news of her death, at her home in Camden, North London, on July 23, 2011, aged just 27.

Chapter One

God Bless The Child

Step out of Southgate's celebrated circular London Underground station and you step out of a time warp. Its brickwork is stained with pollution and years of commuters charging in and out on the pulse of the rush hour. You note a florist, a dry cleaner, an Indian restaurant. You note a blue plastic display bin containing copies of the free weekly newspaper, *The Jewish News*. This is north London, the heart of Jewish London. At the newsagent at the entrance/exit to the station, *The Jewish Chronicle* is sold out. You stand and look at the station. It's a monument, a beautiful London landmark. Designed by Charles Holden, it opened in 1933 and bore all the Art Deco/ Streamline Moderne touches of the time. The station has a sci-fi look to it, like a spaceship from an episode of *The Twilight Zone*. Today, on account of its supreme architectural merits, it's a Grade II-listed building.

The only fast thing in Southgate is the pace of the traffic passing through. The soundtrack is of agitated drivers over-riding clutches and brakes. Bearing left and walking up Chase Side, you take in the distinctive retail landscape of the typical suburban British high street, gathered here collectively under the umbrella of "Southgate

Shopping Centre, London Borough of Enfield". An off-licence, a tapas bar, a Wimpy restaurant, a sandwich bar, a NatWest bank, a charity shop, a gift cards shop, a "cheap clothes" outlet, a restaurant advertising itself as offering "Italian/Indian" cuisine, a Barclay's bank, a Costcutters supermarket, the ubiquitous McDonald's restaurant, an optician's, a kebab shop, a Chinese medicine practice, a florist, a betting shop, a dental practice and so on.

Outside convenience shops, pyramid stacks of avocadoes, papaya, oranges, apples, tomatoes, onions. Inside, shelves heaving with chocolate bars, brands of chewing gum; refrigerated cabinets packed tight with chilled soft drinks. On the magazine stands, the day's national newspapers, this week's local papers, magazines of all kinds, covering all manner of subjects. The date is Tuesday, 12 August, 2007, and all the papers are leading with one story, and it's the story of a Southgate girl turned celebrity. She's on the brink of international stardom and now officially a serious star at home, as much for her calamitous lifestyle as her music. That local girl is, of course, Amy Winehouse, who grew up here in Southgate.

Southgate was originally the South Gate of the King's hunting grounds, Enfield Chase. Becoming independent from Edmonton in 1881, the suburb started to come into its own when nearby Palmer's Green station opened, leading to a population boom. Then, in 1933, when the North Circular Road was completed, it ran through Southgate, connecting the emerging north London suburb to central London. The same year, as the Piccadilly Line pushed ever further outwards, Southgate underground station opened. These developments led to a housing boom, which mostly saw the construction of endless semi-detached houses.

Carrying on up Chase Side, the suburban sprawl continues as you pass estate agents, faded office blocks, Southgate Police Station, a bakery, a post office, the Southgate Club Ltd (members only), a shop selling only products that cost one pound, several pubs, a charity shop with a well-thumbed biography of Princess Diana displayed prominently in the window, a BP petrol station and finally, just off the high street, a large Asda supermarket. Walking further up the hill, there are two houses with the official England Football Team poster in their windows. A wreck of a car is dumped on a grass verge, flat tyres. A bus stop is splashed with graffiti. Two cars in quick succession drive by bombing the neighbourhood with hip-hop.

It was here that Amy Winehouse grew up. Her father Mitchell, then 34, better known as Mitch Winehouse, was a double-glazing salesman. Her mother Janis, 28, a pharmacy technician, had put herself through an Open University science degree and would later go on to study at the London School of Pharmacy. The couple lived in a small two-bedroom flat at the time of Amy's birth, and subsequently moved to a typical Southgate Thirties semi-detached house. Amy was not their first child. They already had a son, Alex, who was born four years earlier, in 1979, when Mitch was 31 and Janis 25.

Their only daughter, Amy Jade Winehouse, was born at Chase Farm hospital in Enfield on September 14, 1983. According to data from 2006, the hospital sees over 500,000 patients per year. A district general hospital, it is located in north Enfield on The Ridgeway. Some of the hospital's buildings hark back to the 19th century, with others having been added since. For instance, in the Seventies, ahead of Amy's birth, a purpose-built building was erected, which thereafter and still today houses the children's services and maternity departments.

Speaking to *The Daily Mail* in 2007, Janis said of Amy as a child, "She was a beautiful child – always busy, always curious. She was always very cheery but she was also shy. She's never been an easy child."

She also mentioned how Amy, even as a child, got into her fair share of scrapes. "As a toddler in her pram she once nearly choked on Cellophane. Another time she went missing in the park. She's tough, like me – I see that as my gift to her."

When Amy was four, she began attending Osidge Primary School in the borough of Barnet. The school, today a two-form entry, grant-maintained primary, is located at Chase Side, Southgate. Children start at the school, in reception class, during the academic year, September to August, in which their fifth birthday falls, and remain at the school until the age of 11, when they transfer to state-funded secondary schools or private schools. Classes number up to 30 children.

The school, heavily oversubscribed, with a waiting list from the age of three, has children of many religions and offers a multi-faith approach to Religious Education. The school also has a strong focus on music education. According to a 2006 inspection report, it had 419 pupils of mixed gender. Many pupils graduate from Osidge Primary School at the age of 11 and move around the corner to continue their studies at Ashmole Secondary School on Cecil Road, also in Southgate.

It was at Osidge that Amy met and became close friends with fellow singer/songwriter Juliette Ashby, as Amy later told *The Observer* in 2007: "We met at Osidge when we were about four. One of my first memories is that we'd play this game where Juliette was Pepsi and I was Shirley, the backing girls for Wham! I think we clicked because we were both a bit off-key." Ashby told *The Observer* how the two of them were always getting into trouble: "I used to egg Amy on a bit more because she was more fearless. One of our best routines was that one of us would run out of the classroom in tears, and the other would say that they'd have to go out and comfort her. And then we'd just sit in a room somewhere, laughing for the rest of the lesson."

Ashby also told *The Observer* what it was like to be friends with Amy: "Amy was always keeping her friends on their toes. I made her a friendship brooch once and she threw it in the sandpit."

For Amy the friendship also had its usual ups and downs: "She was the one with the upper hand. Juliette always had strawberry shoelaces in her bag, and you knew you were flavour of the day if she offered you one."

The girls also shared having an older sibling. Amy, of course, had a brother, Alex, four years her senior. Juliette had a sister, Jessica, three years her senior. Their father, Jonathan Ashby, was the founder of WENN, the World Entertainment News Network. Juliette and Amy have remained close friends to the present day. "Yeah, my best friends are from school when I was growing up," Amy told *Interview* in August 2007. "But I spend all my time with my husband."

Family life at home was not particularly focused on the religious aspects of Judaism, but there was a strong sense of a Jewish cultural identity. For instance, Amy went to Cheder classes every Sunday (where she would have been introduced to the basics of Judaism and the Hebrew language). Not that she liked them.

"Every week I'd say, 'I don't want to go, dad, please don't make me go,'" she told *Totally Jewish* in 2005. "He was so soppy he often let me off. I never learnt anything about being Jewish when I went anyway."

Even though she and her family went to synagogue on Yom Kippur, being Jewish to Amy really meant all things familial. "Being Jewish to me is about being together as a real family. It's not about lighting candles and saying a brachah."

She elaborated on this to *Interview* magazine, saying, "We didn't grow up religious. I'm just a real family girl. I come from a big family. I think it's important to have your family around you, to be close to your family. Having said that, I haven't spoken to my mum or my dad for a week. But I'm very lucky I have a mum and dad."

Growing up, music was always important. Janis remembers how Mitch was always singing to the children and encouraging their interest in music.

"Mitchell and Amy were close," she told *The Daily Mail* in 2007. "Her father would sing Sinatra to her and because he always sang, she was always singing, even in school. Her teachers had to tell her to stop doing it in lessons."

Jazz was in the family tree. Amy's Uncle Leon was a professional horn player, and her paternal grandmother, Cynthie, was once engaged to Ronnie Scott, the saxophonist who founded the now world-famous jazz club in London's Soho. She told *The Sunday Herald* in January 2007, "She was so beautiful. I always say that if Frank Sinatra had seen my nan before Ava Gardner, then I'd be lounge royalty."

While Mitch was always playing the jazz greats, at home and in his car, Janis preferred singer-songwriters such as Carole King and James Taylor. Amy has spoken of how often she used to hear Carole King in her mother's car.

By now, the family had moved to a three-bedroom Victorian house on Osidge Lane, still in Southgate. A leafy residential street situated a five-minute walk up the hill from Asda, it is quiet and tree-lined and the houses are pleasant and spacious. Amy was in the throes of a

Michael Jackson obsession. She later said that she wasn't sure if she wanted to be him or marry him.

Then, when she was nine, her parents separated. Little has been said of the split. Janis gave brief insights into the reasons when speaking with *The Daily Mail* in 2007: "We never argued. We'd had a very agreeable marriage but he was never there. He was a salesman so he was away a lot, but for a long time there was also another woman, Jane, who became his second wife. I think Mitchell would have liked to have both of us but I wasn't happy to do that."

Amy was 10 when Mitch and Janis went their separate ways, with Amy and her brother, by all accounts, going to live with Janis down the road in East Finchley. Janis' mother was constantly on hand to help raise the children, as Janis worked as a pharmacy technician. Amy had said, "Growing up in East Finchley was cool." Much like Southgate, East Finchley, in the neighbouring borough of Barnet, is a North London suburb that first developed in the 19th Century with the construction of the Victorian station, East End, Finchley in 1867. That station was ripped down and replaced by the present London Underground station, East Finchley, in 1939. Like Southgate station, it was designed in the same Art Deco/Streamline Moderne style by Charles Holden. The station is as known today for Holden's iconic look as for Eric Aumonier's statue of an archer aiming his bow up the rail tracks towards central London.

Coming out of East Finchley station today, you wander, as you do from Southgate station, onto a polite parade of suburban North London shops, restaurants and houses. A billboard advertising *The Jewish Chronicle* again reminds you that you're in a typically Jewish part of north London. Walking along, you pass a minicab office, a café, a newsagent, corner shops, convenience shops, a pub, a pharmacy, a dry cleaner, the Phoenix cinema, a florist, an off-licence, a nail studio, a launderette, a betting shop, Finchley Youth Theatre and so on. The parade of shops and restaurants continues for a short distance before blurring into residential streets.

By this time, Amy had moved on from Michael Jackson to Madonna, as she told *Blender* in 2007: "I listened to Madonna's *Immaculate Collection* every day until I was about 11. And then I discovered Salt'N'Pepa and TLC."

She related to the strong, female, opinionated lyrics of both outfits. This was an era when Salt'N'Pepa, an American rap duo, were releasing hit singles like 'Let's Talk About Sex' and 'Whatta Man'. The directness of the lyrics must have struck a chord with Amy. Also, the way men were discussed – Salt'N'Pepa sang honestly – pulled no punches.

"My first real role models were Salt'N'Pepa and Lisa 'Left Eye' Lopes," Amy told *Interview* in 2007. "They were real women who weren't afraid to talk about men and they got what they wanted and talked about girls they didn't like. That was always really cool."

It's particularly interesting that Amy was so intrigued by Lisa 'Left Eye' Lopes. Lopes, best known as a member of massively successful American R&B trio TLC, often got more headlines for her turbulent personal life than she did for the music she made. Notably, in June 1994, she was arrested after setting fire to the $2 million house of her boyfriend, Atlanta Falcons player Andre Rison, after an argument. Charged with arson, she ended up with a $10,000 fine and five years' probation. She also checked into rehab to be treated for alcoholism. Rumours of erratic behaviour continued until her premature death in 2002 in a car accident in Honduras. She was only 30. Lopes shrugged off gossip, saying, "There's a thin line between genius and insanity – and I always get labelled as being the crazy one."

At the time Amy discovered TLC, they would likely have been promoting their second album, *CrazySexyCool*, which featured the hit singles 'Waterfalls' and 'Creep', the latter an account of a woman who still loves her man even though she suspects he's cheating on her: the kind of relationship-wars subject matter that Amy has since made her trademark.

With Juliette Ashby just as smitten with Salt'N'Pepa and TLC, she and Amy formed their own rap duo called Sweet'n'Sour. Amy later said: "We had a tune called 'Spinderella', which was great." She also later described the double act as being, "the little white Jewish Salt'n'Pepa."

At the age of 11, Amy moved up from Osidge Primary School to Ashmole Secondary School, along with Juliette, whose older sister, Jessica, was already there. The school, based at Cecil Road, Southgate, around the corner from Osidge, takes pupils in from the age of 11 and offers a sixth-form education to the age of 18.

That same year, as well as discovering Salt'N'Pepa and TLC, Amy discovered jazz in a major way, as she told *The Guardian* in 2004. "From the age of 11, I was listening to Ella Fitzgerald, who would sing the song perfectly but in a straight way, and then I learnt about subtlety. I heard people like Sarah Vaughan use her voice as an instrument and that inspired me so much because it made me realise that a whisper can be so much more effective than just belting something out."

Meanwhile, Amy missed her father being around. The matter of her parents' separation was solidified when they formally divorced, when she was 12. "People talk a lot about the anger in Amy's songs," her mother told *The Daily Mail* later. "I think a lot of it was that her father wasn't there."

Having been a natural and eager performer to date – appearing in school plays and local amateur youth productions – Amy took it on herself to apply to Sylvia Young Theatre School in central London – "a specialist, Performing Arts School". The school, located at Rossmore Road, Marylebone, takes pupils in at either age 10 or 11. The admissions process is strict, as their website states: "All prospective students will be invited to a workshop audition where, as part of a group, they will be invited to take part in a Drama, Singing and Dance class." After the first audition, school reports are taken into consideration and a second audition/interview takes place, featuring an English test and a maths test, as well as various acting, song and dance tests. The school insists that while it is a theatre school, its pupils must also graduate with a solid, broad education. The admissions process is incredibly competitive and there are very few scholarships. Today, for regular students, fees for year six are £2,150 per term. For years seven, eight and nine, the fees per term are £2,900. For years 10 and 11, the fees hit £3,000 per term.

Janis Winehouse told *The Daily Mail* about the sudden circumstances that led to her daughter applying to Sylvia Young's, landing a prestigious scholarship and leaving Ashmole school. "At about the same time, my mother-in-law and I took the kids to Cyprus on holiday. There was a talent show and Amy really wanted to enter it. She did and we sat there listening to her and I think that's when I knew that she had something really special. But I would have been happy for her to stay at the local school where she had been before."

In an interview with *The Daily Mail* in 2007, Sylvia Young wrote of Amy's audition, "It is hard to overstate just how much she struck me as unique, both as a composer and performer, from the moment she first came through the doors at the age of 13, sporting the same distinctive hairstyle that she has now. Her abilities could put her in the same league as Judy Garland or Ella Fitzgerald."

Once she was awarded the scholarship in spring 1997, she began what would be a three-year stint studying at Sylvia Young's. Soon after starting, she became good friends with a singer/songwriter called Tyler James, while others studying there at the time included Billie Piper and Matt Willis, who would go on to be a member of the band Busted. Of her time there Amy told *The Independent* in 2004, "They had us singing *Flashdance* and all stuff from musicals, 'Where Is Love', cheesy stuff like that. But if we ever had a jazzy song or a sexy, husky song they'd always give me a solo in that."

Despite loving the performing arts side of the curriculum, Amy struggled with her academic studies, having a hard time focusing. When she wasn't interested, she tended to shut down and misbehave, as Sylvia Young recalled when writing for *The Daily Mail*. "She wouldn't wear the school uniform correctly. She chewed gum in lessons. She wore a silver nose-ring and, when I asked her to take it out, she apologised, removed it, and replaced it an hour later. I could not ignore it but I understood and we found a way of coexisting. She would break the rules; I would tell her off; and she would acknowledge it. She could be disruptive in class, too, but this was largely because she didn't concentrate. She was, as I have said, wonderfully clever – so much so that we decided to move her one year ahead of her age group in the hope she would feel more challenged. Despite this, she was often bored out of her mind, although not in English lessons, which she loved."

Meanwhile, early signs of a predisposition to depression were beginning to emerge. Amy told *Rolling Stone* in 2007, "I do suffer from depression, I suppose. Which isn't that unusual. You know, a lot of people do. But I think because I had an older brother, I did a lot of that, 'Oh life's so depressing' stuff before I was even twelve. That's when I would be reading J.D. Salinger – or whatever my brother read – and feeling frustrated."

Earlier, when she was nine, she had harmed herself deliberately, a common symptom of clinical depression. "It's a funny thing, a morbid curiosity," she told Q magazine in 2007. "I'm talking about when I was nine. What does that feel like? Ow, that fucking hurts. It's probably the worst thing I've done."

One evening, hiding away in her room, feeling miserable, she had an epiphany while lying morose on her bed. Through the wall she heard a wonderful piece of music that lifted her spirits, offered her comfort, a point to relate to. Her brother was listening to ''Round Midnight', the jazz classic. Amy heard it, loved it, and embarked on a voyage to discover all the great jazz singers and musicians. "I learnt from Ella Fitzgerald and Sarah Vaughan and Dinah Washington," she told *The Independent* in 2004. "They were the most inspiring people to me when I was developing a voice. It was the first real music apart from hip-hop that ever spoke to me and made an emotional connection."

When she was 14, the studies at Sylvia Young's paid off and Amy made her first TV appearance on *The Fast Show*, playing a character in a sketch called 'Peasblossom'. The episode (Season Three, Episode Two) first aired on November 21 1997, and her credit is logged at imdb.com.

Parallel to her love of music, she also developed a serious interest in film. She later told *The Independent* in 2004 what kinds of films she was watching during this era: "*It's A Wonderful Life*, Hitchcock's *Vertigo*, *Dirty Dancing*, *From Here To Eternity*. Why do I love them? How long have you got? I'd be in film studies if I could. I could write you an essay on them."

Musically, she was getting into hip-hop and R&B in a major way. The 1997 debut album by a new female American artist particularly caught her attention. *Baduizm*, by Erykah Badu, would prove to be a definitive influence on the soundscapes of Amy's forthcoming debut album *Frank*. A mix of urban soul, jazz and R&B, the album led to many comparisons with the ghost of Billie Holiday. Amy's debut album would definitely aim for a similar space in music, somewhere between contemporary black urban American music and the legendary pastures of jazz.

A year later, in 1998, another American album caught Amy's attention and left her mesmerised. That album was *Mos Def & Talib Kweli Are Black Star*, by rappers Mos Def and Talib Kweli. Several articles about Winehouse have also mentioned a "boyfriend with a heavy reggae habit" during this period of her life, and he in turn introduced her to reggae, presumably opening the door for that influence to also form part of *Frank*'s eclectic sound.

Then, that same year, her mother received a call from Sylvia Young's, asking her to come in for a meeting about her daughter. In a 2007 interview with *The Daily Mail*, Janis revealed what happened: "The principal phoned up and asked me to come in and see him. He said, I think you should take her away. He didn't want children who weren't going to get good grades and Amy wasn't going to. She was very bright but she was always messing around. The same day, I had to take the family cat Katie to the vet. I dropped off the cat, went to the school and then went back to the vet's. We had the cat put down. My joke is I should have had Amy put down and the cat moved on."

Sylvia Young, in turn, in an article for *The Daily Mail* in 2007, denied that her school expelled Amy. She explained that the then academic head had called Amy's mother and informed her that she was on course to fail her GCSEs on account of her being too easily distracted. "As a result of the conversation Amy's mother decided to send her elsewhere. I was very unhappy to discover this and the teacher who made the call left us shortly afterwards."

Despite the break, Sylvia Young kept her connection with Amy. "I didn't want to break my ties with her and kept in touch, perhaps to her surprise given our disagreements over the rules. When she reached 16, I arranged for her to audition for the National Youth Jazz Orchestra. She was later spotted performing with the Orchestra by colleagues of pop manager Simon Fuller, the man who was behind the Spice Girls' success."

For now, though, Amy was devastated at having been taken out of Sylvia Young's. She has said that she cried every night after leaving, and apparently found solace in the music of Ray Charles. As her parents set about arranging a new school, Amy would spend the best part of the following year obsessively listening to Charles, parallel to her ongoing hip-hop and R&B infatuations.

Her parents settled on The Mount school in Mill Hill, an independent day school for girls from aged four to 18. Today, the school has around 400 pupils – approximately 100 aged four to 11 and 300 aged 11 to 18 – and is based at Milespit Hill. The school was founded in 1925 in Highgate by Mary McGregor and, ten years later, moved to its present campus in Mill Hill. The school's motto is *Esse quam videre* – "to be rather than to seem to be". The school is non-denominational in its approach and has pupils of all faiths, an important issue to the Jewish Winehouses. If Amy were 13 and going to The Mount today, the school fees per term would be £3,175. It offers extra-curricular music lessons, with opportunities to learn piano, clarinet, the flute, saxophone, violin and guitar. All of these music lessons cost extra to the basic school fees per term.

Amy did not like The Mount very much and studied through an unhappy year, graduating in 1996, at the age of 16, with five GCSEs. Briefly, according to popular myth, she coasted through a run of short-lived jobs – working in a piercing shop, a tattoo parlor and a clothes shop – before refocusing her sights on another performing arts school, this time the BRIT Performing Arts & Technology School in Croydon, which charges students no fees.

Students at the BRIT school are admitted at either age 14 or 16. It bills itself as "Britain's only FREE Performing Arts & Technology School", and Amy went there for a barely a year before dropping out. Adrian Packer, head of the Musical Theatre department, told *The Independent* in 2007 that teaching Amy was, "Exciting but nerve-racking. She was an artist from the age of 16 and she wasn't exactly suited to being institutionalised."

While Any was studying at the BRIT School, Sylvia Young arranged for her to audition with the National Youth Jazz Orchestra. Blown away by her amazing voice, the Orchestra took her on and she began singing at jazz clubs.

Meanwhile, leisure time meant hanging out with Juliette Ashby and getting stoned, as she told *The Observer* in 2007. "We always met at my house when we got to about 16 and started smoking dope."

Having either left or quit the BRIT school (depending on which account of her education you choose to go with) and sure of her destiny to be a singer and songwriter, she threw her all into the gigs with the National Youth Jazz Orchestra. By now aged 17, she also needed to earn some money, and a timely offer of employment came from best friend Juliette, who fixed it with her father that she and Amy could work for WENN. Amy tried her hand at what she has variously called either showbiz or music journalism and held down the job for around three months. With offices in London, Los Angeles, Las Vegas and various other prime cities, the job with WENN would be regarded by many as a heaven-sent opportunity to ease yourself into the glamorous world of popular culture, but, instead of enjoying the work, Amy found reporting uninspiring and dreamed all the harder of getting home at the end of the day to sing and write songs on her guitar.

The highlights of the week continued to be the weekend gigs with the National Youth Jazz Orchestra. She described this era to *The Sunday Tribune* in January 2007 as follows: "I wanted to be a journalist. I was studying journalism and doing gigs on the weekend. I did my apprenticeship and wrote for them for a bit and then just wanted to do reception. I wanted to do more diverse stuff. I've always been like that, changing things. I'm not a proud person in that way – I have no problem making someone a cup of tea."

One unexpected benefit of the job that wouldn't manifest itself for some time was a chance encounter with a man who was seven years older than Amy. They hit it off and started dating, and the relationship lasted nine months. It was by all accounts Amy's first serious relationship. When the relationship crumbled, the break-up led to some soul-searching on Amy's part and would eventually inform many of the songs on *Frank*.

"I constantly want to look after people," she told *The Observer* in 2006. "But I've only met a couple of men in my life who deserved or appreciated it. My first proper long term boyfriend Chris, the fella that I wrote my first album about, was lovely, but he didn't really appreciate it."

It was by now 2001 and Amy was restless for something to happen. The spark arrived when Tyler James, her friend and fellow aspiring singer/songwriter from Sylvia Young's days, was signed to Brilliant, a division of 19 Management Ltd, the talent agency owned by Simon Fuller and responsible for hurtling The Spice Girls to global success. With a management deal in place, Tyler then set about writing original material. During this time, having stayed close friends with Amy, he knew how she was developing her voice and helped her cut a few demos. He then passed a cassette to an A&R at Brilliant 19 Ltd, Nick Shymansky, who, along with a manager at the firm, Nick Godwin, was on the lookout for a jazz vocalist (perhaps inspired by news that Norah Jones had been signed to Blue Note Records in January 2001).

"We put it on," Godwin told *The Guardian* in 2004. "And there was this amazing voice, fantastic lyrics. They were eight or nine minute poems, really. Quite awkward guitar playing, but utterly breathtaking."

Shymansky felt the same and arranged through Tyler James to see Amy sing live with the National Youth Jazz Orchestra. A date was made and, as she has done time and time again ever since, despite the inevitable pressure of singing before an A&R man who could fast-track her career depending on her performance, she took to the stage and sang her heart out. Shymansky was blown away and made his approach. Over the coming weeks, he told her that Brilliant 19 Ltd was interesting in managing her. Amy couldn't believe her luck.

"I didn't go knocking on people's doors," she told *The Belfast Telegraph* in February 2007. "I wouldn't bother sending anybody your tape. People get tapes by the sackload and a lot of the time they don't care."

Shymansky decided that the best plan would be to have Amy write some original songs with a collaborator and cut some serious demos, which could be used to court record label interest. Knowing that Amy had many influences – from TLC, Mos Def and The Beastie Boys through to Ella Fitzgerald, Sarah Vaughan and Frank Sinatra – he

figured it might be interesting to start by hooking her up with a producer with a feel for an urban sound, someone who could try setting
her jazzy vocal style in a more contemporary context. Amy had mentioned that she was working on some songs with a guitar player – and
that the guitar player had a west London producer friend who went
by the name of Major. Shymansky checked Major out and, on learning that *NME* had said of him – "he creates a backing track unlike
any other" – dialled his number in early September 2001.

Chapter Two

Wild Is The Wind

Major was the perfect man for the job and had the qualities Nick Shymansky was looking for. If he could bring a perfect backing track to Amy's perfect voice, then they'd have magic. Major was keen and hungry and had an edge, too. Ditto Amy. He had a creative approach to production and was not a producer who simply recorded sound. Major was the kind of producer who collaborated with the artist, co-wrote, co-arranged, embellished, pushed, knew how to expand a beat or melody into something exciting, different. In this hook-up, Shymansky seemed to have understood right from the start that Amy would work best with a producer who helped her craft and honed her songs. And so Major began a tradition that would later draw in Salaam Remi and Mark Ronson.

Major was born and raised in west London, and grew up soaking up the eclectic sounds of the neighbourhood. Reggae was a natural love, since his stepfather had a sound system and instructed him in the basics of DJ'ing when he was in his teens. The first record Major ever bought was Junior Murvin's 'Police And Thieves' – a reggae classic and a crossover hit when covered by The Clash. Once he had mastered DJ'ing and operating a sound system, Major went on the road touring with sound systems such as Calvary, Lethal Weapon, One Love and Heartbeat. From there, he moved on to MC'ing on stage at the MOBO award-winning club night, Rotation. He also worked extensively across the British club scene, alongside DJs such as Ras Kwame (Radio 1), Tony Touch, Femi Fem and Dodge (MTV), and hosted parties for the likes of *Touch* magazine and P. Diddy.

At the time he got the call from Shymansky, Major had moved into producing after a chance encounter with Howie B. He and Major crossed paths when working in the same studio. They got along, formed a friendship, and when Howie B went away travelling he gave Major the keys to his studio. Never having had free reign in a studio before, Major spent the time experimenting feverishly. He played some of the results of his experimentation to trip-hop star Tricky, who was impressed enough to pay for Major to go into a studio with Zoe, a young female artist Tricky was nurturing. Tricky wanted Major to work on some tracks with Zoe for potential release on his label. The sessions went well and Major walked away feeling that what got him excited was working with fresh talent. He liked the excitement of curating a talent in bloom.

When Shymansky called, Major heard him out and said he was definitely interested. They agreed to meet and set a date: September 11, 2001. When the day came round, it became one that Major would not forget for two reasons. One, because the meeting led to him working with Amy Winehouse, and two, because of the terrorist attacks on the World Trade Center, which rocked the world that day.

"I'll never forget the day I went to meet Nick at 19 to discuss whether I wanted to work with Amy or not," remembers Major, speaking from his home in Hampstead Garden Suburb. "Because it was 9/11. I remember that morning I watched the 9/11 attacks and then I went to my meeting. On the way down I was staring at the sky thinking, 'Any minute now'."

When he arrived at the meeting, everyone was talking about what had happened in New York, just as everyone in the western world with access to TV and media was talking about the same thing. When they'd finished airing the subject, Shymansky played him some demos of Amy singing and then presented the project to him.

"At this time, Amy was just demoing with a few people here and there and Nick was like, do you wanna work with her? And I heard her stuff and was like, yeah, definitely. Nick was just trying to say to me, look, if you listen to her, you can hear where she's going."

Feeling that Major definitely got the vibe of Amy's voice, where she was coming from, where she wanted to go, Shymansky arranged for Amy and Major to meet at the latter's then home studio in Kensal Rise, roughly a week after the events of September 11.

"She just wanted something a little bit different," Major recalls of their first encounter. "And I also knew she was very kinda' street as well, because she loved hip-hop, she loved R&B, she loved all that kind of stuff. So originally we went down that route."

They worked on material, with Amy singing and Major working up some beats for her. That first meeting generated new demo tracks. What struck Major most was her ability to conjure spontaneous magic. A few days later, that magic came alive even more spectacularly.

"One day I phoned up, after I demoed her, and we did about four tracks. One of the songs was called 'Alcoholic Logic'. She was in Southampton that weekend and I done this beat and I played it down the phone to her, because she was on her way to my house at the time on the train. By the time she got to my house, within 20 minutes, half hour, we'd finished recording the whole thing. She wrote it on the train, on her way to mine. She basically just wrote up her weekend, what she did."

This knack for honestly documenting the things that occur in her life would become Amy's trademark. Major quickly noticed how she worked best. If they tried working too hard on material, nothing happened. If he just let things happen, then she'd periodically come out with something spectacular. In any case, the excitement over the speed and ease with which 'Alcoholic Logic' came together bonded producer and artist, and the sessions remained intimate thereafter. Typically, it was just Amy working with Major, but eventually they brought in a guitarist to embellish certain songs.

"On one or two of the tracks we got in Ian Barter, who played some of the guitar. He actually taught her how to play the guitar. He was quite a key person in what I was doing. At this time, she'd just come in and lay the vocal."

From the second they met, Major knew that vintage references were lurking in Amy's vocal style and technique, and that if these were married to a contemporary street edge, then she'd have a unique sound.

"I couldn't really compare her to anyone, I just loved what she was doing. At the time, I was listening to quite a bit of old Nina Simone stuff and when Amy came along, it was like, you need to do stuff from that era, but make it today. I didn't wanna influence Amy by playing her that stuff. I just wanted her to do what she wanted to do but, in my mind, I had the route I wanted to go with her."

The demo sessions were stripped down, rugged, but Major could hear a success story in the making.

"At this point, I was feeling like she would just do it. It was quite weird, quite raw, but it just worked. I didn't really want her to go and perfect it, I wanted it to stay as raw as it was. So she'd come in, put it down, we'd listen to it, we might redo the verse, just to change up some of the words, but that was it."

Mostly, Major did his best to frame Amy's gift for the spontaneous moment, to underline how luminous her delivery was when she was in the mood. "For me, Amy is just a bag of talent. There's not many people I know I can give a beat to there and then and she can write a song just there and then, done. Most people will take it, go away and sit there for hours and hours, but she'd just be vibeing, singing along and next thing I know, it's done. And all that attitude that she had with it as well, it was just good. She had that like quite naturally. It's within her personality to be like that, with what she's doing musically. She's one of them people that you can't really put her in a room and say, sing it like this. She'll sing it like Amy. She's just a very, very natural talent."

Working together, Major insists that Amy's attitude made her strong, bold. She was not intimidated in any way by working with an MC and emerging producer whose CV at the time included work with Soul II Soul and Horace Andy. "No, Amy wasn't nervous at all. She had the most confidence. She weren't nervous and if she was, I didn't know it."

Shymansky was happy with the results, liked the urban feel Major was giving Amy. And Amy, a big fan of Mos Def and The Roots at the time, felt Major understood her twin leanings towards jazz and hip-hop. The next step in Amy's career, according to Major, was instigated by him.

"I kind of hooked her up to get the deal she got. Well, I didn't actually hook her up, but what I did, I was good friends with Darcus Beese at Island Records and I played him one of the songs down the phone. He went mad, he was like, 'Can I meet her? Don't tell her who I am. I'm just going to come over, have a little chill-out with you guys to see what's up. I'm gonna come in as a friend basically, not as an A&R guy. And don't tell her what I do.'"

According to Major, Beese, then, as now, a powerful A&R figure in the British music business, asked for the covert meeting to be arranged as soon as possible.

"And so Darcus came over, heard her sing and within a few weeks of that, there was a deal sealed on the table. And that was it, really. Then she signed and she basically didn't actually start doing any work for a year. And I was off in Australia at the time, touring with Soul II Soul."

As with many details of the Amy Winehouse story, there are various accounts of how Beese came to sign her. In *Spin* magazine's July 2007 Amy cover story, it was reported that Beese, after hearing Major's demos, then visited the 19 Management offices.

"I snuck into the 19 offices to find out who was handling her," Beese is quoted as saying in *Spin*. "Because they were keeping her a secret. I never heard a woman who lyrically put the shit together like she did and I had to have her, so we did the deal. She's Etta James, she's Aretha Franklin, she's Mahalia Jackson, she's Courtney Love."

Other accounts state that Shymansky and 19 Management had discreetly circulated the demos and that there was a race between two or three labels to sign Amy. And that Beese, having a head start through Major and having met Amy informally, was able to get there first. Regardless of whether other labels were chasing Amy, Beese got his girl and the negotiations began. But not only on the strength of the demos. Amy was also asked to come into Island's offices in 2002 and sing before an intimidating spread of the label's bosses. As depicted in the documentary *I Told You I Was Trouble*, she sat charismatically in an armchair, wearing a shirt, jeans and boots and, backed by a male musician playing acoustic guitar, sang exquisitely. Darcus Beese says in the documentary that his colleagues were blown away by her voice and presence too, and they all felt that he was right, she was a potentially phenomenal artist in the making, even if she was yet to find her own unique groove.

Then, there's an account of how she ended up signed to Island that had the following chronology: Shymansky hooked her up with Major, Major tipped off Darcus Beese, Beese met Amy, and Beese stayed tight to Shymansky and Nick Godwin at Brilliant 19 Ltd, which was honing Amy further to ensure a bigger recording contract. Having tested the water label-wise, they then decided to send Amy to write material for what would be her debut album with a team of young songwriters. While Amy worked on the material, Brilliant 19 Ltd discreetly courted one or two other prominent A&Rs at major labels who were also keen to sign her. By autumn 2002, with Amy having worked all spring and summer writing, Godwin opened final negotiations with Darcus Beese at Universal–Island Records. This line of events is confirmed by Stefan Skarbek, one of the songwriters that Godwin arranged for Amy to work with at Mayfair Studios in London.

In the interim, between working with Major and signing on the dotted line with Island, Amy's manager at Brilliant 19 Ltd, Nick Godwin, arranged for her to start working with a pair of young songwriters – Skarbek and Matt Rowe. At the ame time, she was playing tiny pub gigs at venues like the Dublin Castle in her adopted home neighbourhood of Camden, where on certain nights emerging artists could sneak a lucky break and take to the stage to test-drive songs. She always performed with her guitar, very simply, singer-songwriter style.

Amy clicked straight away with Skarbek and Rowe and the trio were booked indefinitely into Mayfair Studios in spring 2002, to begin writing and demoing potential original material that, in theory, would inform the content and direction of her debut album. Occasionally, they were joined by a third songwriter – Felix Howard.

Amy Winehouse, the twenty year old who sings like a forty year old, like Billie Holiday and Nina Simone duetting across time and music history with Lauryn Hill and Erykah Badu. (JAY BROOKS/IDOLS)

Amy, age one. (WENN)

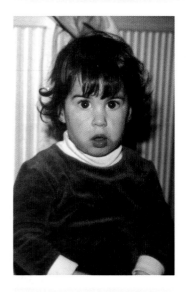

Amy very much resembled her mother, a pharmacist. (REX FEATURES)

Amy at the age of four with her older brother, Alex. (WENN)

Amy at the dinner table, with her brother Alex on the far left, and a friend in the centre. (WENN)

A smiling Amy, age seven, clutching toys, with her brother Alex and their grandparents. (WENN)

The Sylvia Young Theatre School in Marylebone, in central London where Amy studied for three years. (BILLY EASTER)

Amy aged 15, recording a song with best friend Juliette Ashby. The pair once formed a rap duo called Sweet'N'Sour in homage to Salt'N'Pepa. Amy was Sour. (WENN)

The BRIT Performing Arts & Technology School in Croydon, which Amy attended briefly in her mid-teens. "Her time with us, although short, was happy and we are always very pleased to see her doing well," says the Principal, Nick Williams.

Amy signs records for fans at the Virgin Megastore in London's Oxford Street, December 4, 2003. (DAVID BUTLER/REX FEATURES)

Amy performing at the Brits shortlist event on January 12, 2004. (LFI)

Amy with Bobby Womack at the Ivor Novello awards, May 27, 2004. She won the award for the best contemporary song. (LFI)

Amy backstage at the V festival, August 21, 2004. (BIGPICTURESPHOTO.COM)

Amy on stage at the V festival. (DAVID BUTLER/REX FEATURES)

Amy arriving at the Mercury Music Awards in London, September 7, 2004. (LFI)

Amy performing at the Miller Strat Pack concert at Wembley Arena, celebrating 50 years of the Stratocaster, September 23, 2004. (RICHARD YOUNG/REX FEATURES)

Amy with her brother Alex at the wheel, July 14, 2005. (BIGPICTURESPHOTO.COM)

Amy, on the brink of success. "When she showed up for our first session she was wearing a pair of jeans that had completely fallen apart with I Love Sinatra embroidered on the arse," says songwriter Felix Howard. "That's so Amy. I just fell in love with her."

"When she showed up for our first session she was wearing a pair of jeans that had completely fallen apart with I Love Sinatra embroidered on the arse," Howard told *The Guardian* in 2004. "That's so Amy. I just fell in love with her."

Skarbek and Rowe were equally taken with Amy and fell into working with her, occasionally with Howard's input, very organically. "Amy came to us from her management," recalls Skarbek, who has gone on to write for Mel C of The Spice Girls and Alex Parks while fronting his own band, today based in Los Angeles. "A guy called Nick Godwin. She was brought to us very, very early on. I think we were among the first people she ever worked with. And we did a bunch of stuff, we basically did a whole record, and it was really sort of experimental but it was really good fun."

During the early part of 2002 and reaching into summer, they worked on material, messing about, writing and recording sporadically.

"We had great times. For Amy, it was definitely where a lot of the ideas that she's got now sort of flourished. The sound. We never had the tools to do what she went on to do because of one thing and another. But she just came to us and we wrote and pretty much did a whole album."

As the original material piled up, watched over by Godwin, pressure began to bear down on them regarding the sound of the material. Keen to keep steering Amy towards the best possible recording contract, and knowing that the Major demos had created serious interest already, notably from Darcus Beese, Godwin was after a clutch of dazzling, jazzy, bluesy, original, contemporary songs that also checked Amy's hip-hop/R&B influences, in preparation of a deal being struck. Whichever label she went with, Godwin wanted her to go straight to work on her debut album.

"We ended up recording quite a few songs for the first record and then there were some problems with production. So there was a time where there were three producers producing the same record. And to be honest, Amy was caught in it all. I don't think it was the way she wanted to do things at all. It was a bit of mismanagement and a bit of this, that and the other, but we ended up recording quite a few songs.

It went from singles to nothing to having what we had in the end."

Skarbek says a lot of the material had a vivid sense of humour and came out of hours of goofing about. These songs contrasted strongly with the far darker, more serious mood that ended up driving *Frank*.

"I think a lot of the more comical, funny side of Amy is what we did at the beginning, you know, like, 'Amy Amy Amy', all that kind of stuff. I mean, she'd come for weeks at a time and we'd just go off. Most of the time we'd go clothes shopping with her and end up back at the studio on Friday afternoon at three o'clock, and management are coming down at six, so we just wrote and cobbled something together and they'd come down and go, 'Wow, how'd you do all that in a week?' And we're like, 'Actually, we spent most of the time record shopping in Camden or whatever'."

That record shopping summed up the collective mood of musical excitement. The three of them were discovering new music all the time, exploring sounds, then importing them as brand new influences into the music they were writing.

"I was probably still listening to The Beastie Boys," remembers Skarbek. "And that kind of raucousness. When we'd go record shopping in Camden, we used to go and scoop up literally bundles of records and take them back to the studio and sit and listen, sit there and make cups of tea. Which Amy does very well. She makes a mighty fine cup of tea. She used to make like, 20 a day for everyone. By the end, everyone's like, 'Amy enough!'"

Mostly, they were buying blind.

"We were listening to a lot of really weird records. Can you imagine what we were picking up at Oxfam in Kentish Town? We were listening to some pretty out-there stuff, not always jazz. Amy was always into a lot of stuff and I was too, so we'd always find something that we'd like to listen to and then we'd listen to, it over and over and sit there and jam out. We'd also do things like go to the zoo and claim to be at work. And then rush back and try and cobble something together, which the record company actually thought was amazing. At that point, it was more for the love of it than anything else."

The era was also one when Amy the musician was learning all the time, picking up new instruments, hungry for as many outlets and channels for her talent as possible. For instance, she asked Skarbek to teach her how to play the trumpet, which led to some amusing scenes at Mayfair Studios.

"She was obsessed with playing the trumpet, so she used to go outside the room with it when we were noodling about and I'd teach her how to play a scale. You'd get the other people who were in the studio wondering what was going on. One time I think Madonna was there, and she sent someone up just to find out where this awful noise was coming from, and it was Amy in the corridor trying to do a scale on the trumpet. It was always very much a laugh."

Skarbek says the sessions were primarily about fun and, out of the relaxed atmosphere, they happened upon gem-like musical moments quite by accident, never forcing composition, always letting the moment take them.

"I was working with Matt Rowe and occasionally with Felix Howard and it was like a sort of family vibe. It wasn't the clinical studio environment that you might have thought. It was very much more a case of we did what we felt like when we wanted to do it. It was great."

One such magic moment led to the off-the-cuff writing of 'Amy Amy Amy', a woozy, jazzy track that made its way onto her debut album. "Amy came to the studio one day and she had a boyfriend at the time who we called mushy peas, because he always used to come to our studio to pick her up with chips and mushy peas from the local fish shop. And then we had a little backing vocal section, which was me, Matt and Felix, and we called ourselves The Cheesy Peas in honour of him. Anyway, she turned up and told me some story about doing whatever, not calling him back or dumping him and I said, 'oh Amy Amy Amy' and it sprung into that song. That's how it happened, as organic as you like."

Skarbek says that many of her songs evolved this way, riffing off an expression *du jour*, a playful turn of phrase doing the rounds in their inner circle. Word games became lyrics that sparkled.

"It usually came from something we'd say. A lot of the other songs – which I personally think are the unsung heroes of her stuff, they're the ones that I'd really love to hear out in the open – came out of nowhere. There's one called 'I'm A Monkey Not A Boy', another we did called 'Ease Up On Me'. We did all these songs and they were very much right there and then. We'd always write with her, but the lead would come from her. She would not sing anything she was not into. You can gauge it in her shoulders, if they start rising, then you know she's getting cringe factor and, at that point, she's not enjoying it."

Another song, called 'The Ambulance Man', also came out of thin air.

"Amy's gran had fallen ill and Amy came in the studio at midday, literally turned on the mic while I sat at the piano and we just recorded this song. It was like she'd just had it in her head. Or it just came to her. She was just connecting with something pretty high and mighty there, you know. She just came and wrote the whole song. It was really silly but also kind of deep. It was definitely multi-layered. All of her stuff has an uncanny way of being like that. Her voice is her voice, you've heard it. But for me, it's much more about what's behind each word and each thing that she's talking about. That's what makes her unique."

No matter how good the mood was, how rich the creative pastures, as a deal with Island Records looked increasingly likely there was a need for a clear sound, a unified direction, a concerted push towards a body of material that would make for a potent debut album.

"Amy was at that point unsure," recalls Skarbek. "She knew roughly what she wanted to do, but she was being told to do other things. There was no hope in hell that that sort of a jazz singer would cut it. But she was probably the only person I've ever worked with who basically said, a big two fingers to it, I'm gonna do what I wanna do."

That wilfulness meant the three of them could continue with the hi-jinks and good times. "By summer time, we'd be up on Primrose Hill drinking white Russians. That was our favourite pastime."

And then, the party came to an end. "Summer 2002 was when the politics of it all came to a head a bit," says Skarbek. "Because we were supposed to make the record. And I guess it was about that summer that suddenly a lot of tracks were put on the back-burner, purely because of the production stuff."

The production issue affected most of the tracks that Amy had composed with Skarbek and Rowe. Along with the question mark over the quality of the recordings, Skarbek also sensed a change in Amy the artist and where she wanted to go with her music.

"To be honest, she'd probably matured, she didn't want to sing about monkeys and stuff like that any more. I think that's probably what happened. But that summer I remember quite clearly that we had three studios running at Mayfair Studios. We'd booked three places and there were three producers. And then, at that point, I think they (Amy's management) wanted it more accessible and not a sort of comedy record, because they needed to break it out."

Eventually, only two tracks from the sessions made it onto her debut album – 'Amy Amy Amy' and 'October Song'. Skarbek recalls clearly the day he and Amy wrote 'October Song', a track inspired by the death of her pet canary.

"Amy went away for the weekend and forgot to feed her canary. And decided to write a song about it. I don't think the canary died because she didn't feed it. I think it died anyway. So we wrote the song. She was always very much up for doing the writing there and then, which I love. She was great to work with and it was always fun. We did many, many melodies."

Looking back now, Skarbek has a clear take on the feel of the songs they worked on that spring and summer. "They're really wacky, but really funny. Some of the songs that we've done keep threatening to come back. The B-side to 'Rehab', 'Do Me Good', that's a song we did as well."

Today he thinks that the wacky, funny material, while part of Amy's personality, clashed with the image she had for her future. "There is a thing in her, which is like, she's scared of that lighter side of her more than she is of the serious jazz singer. She definitely wants to be and aspires to be that serious jazz singer, Sarah Vaughan, Ella Fitzgerald, all of those people."

Skarbek also sees signs in those sessions of the Amy Winehouse we know today. "Being a trumpet player myself, doing stuff with her on

'Amy Amy Amy' and her getting into it, that probably planted the seed for her to want to have the big brass stuff going on. Then, with us doing the funny backing vocal things that we used to do as The Cheesy Peas, it was like a kinda Twenties thing, that slightly burlesquey kinda stuff, three cheesy guys in the background doing a little dance and singing. She's sort of taken that on a bit. I went and saw her in LA not long ago, this year (2007), and she had a bunch of guys doing exactly that, but they were better than we were."

By the time the sessions came to a natural end, Nick Godwin at Brilliant 19 Ltd was working manager's magic, securing a publishing deal for Amy with EMI Music Publishing Ltd. The advance from the deal, for Amy, meant financial independence. Amy, now 18, straight away moved into a flat in Camden with her best friend Juliette Ashby. Speaking to *The Observer* in 2007, Juliette said of their time living together, "I've got such brilliant memories of that flat. I'd have passed out from being stoned and Amy would be roasting a chicken at three in the morning. When she's stressed, or a bit fucked up in the head, Amy'll be in the kitchen. She loves feeding people. She's a nutcase, but she's a good person. I worry for her a lot. There have been nights when I've been in bed and I've heard this banging sound."

Asked at the same time by the paper what Juliette might have heard, Amy said, "Me, banging my head against the wall. I don't do that so much these days."

By the autumn, Godwin was closing down a deal with Darcus Beese.

Did Skarbek lament the change of direction that meant they stopped writing with Amy? "I would say that we grew together. I know that she looks back on that time and she loved it and it was great fun, but I think there was a point where she was scared of that side of her a bit and she wanted to get her serious licks out."

Then, finally, at the end of the year, a deal was struck. On December 17, 2002, Amy Winehouse, at the tender age of 19, was officially signed to Universal–Island Records.

Chapter Three

I Put A Spell On You

Although some songs were already in the bag – 'October Song' and 'Amy Amy Amy' for instance – Island's first impulse was to set Amy up right away with a producer who could take her sound to a new level. Darcus Beese knew how well Amy had responded to a producer-collaborator like Major, and must also have noted how blurred the focus got when there was no dedicated producer working on material at Mayfair Studios. Knowing that Amy had been listening a lot to the American rapper Nas, Beese decided to check out the possibility of her working with Miami-based producer Salaam Remi, who had worked with Nas. An additional reason why Beese thought Remi and Amy might work well together was that Remi had recently produced *A Little Deeper*, the 2002 debut album by the London R&B singer, which included the hit single 'Dy-na-mi-tee'.

Parallel to the label deciding on which producer to use, Amy's relationship with Chris, the older boyfriend she had met at WENN, had come to an end. Miserable that he had broken off the relationship with her, Amy retreated and, as would happen again with *Back To Black*, found herself feverishly writing songs about the experience.

"When my first boyfriend split up with me, it was something I really couldn't make sense of," she told *The Sunday Herald* in 2007, reflecting on the inspiration for the *Frank* album. "I didn't understand why. So I wrote 'Take The Box', about how I literally had to put all his stuff in a box and get rid of it. That's a good example of how that sorted me out."

Working with that heartache, within no time she had crafted a bag of originals with which she could go into the studio. As she was quickly learning, songwriting was very cathartic. She poured her upset into music, made great music, pain over. Everybody wins. The only downside was that she needed to have bad things happen to her in order to feel sad enough to write from the heart, as she noted to *The Times* in 2003: "Being a musician and a singer, there is always going to be something in me that is completely twisted, fucked up and sad. But I don't want to be stuck in a room where all I ever do is write: lie there and cry and then write a song."

Writing openly and candidly and from first-hand experience was what came naturally. Amy's confessional songwriting style – inspired no doubt by growing up in a home where her mother was always playing the classic soul-baring singer-songwriters James Taylor and Carole King – was to fit the Oprah Winfrey/*Sex And The City*/*Prozac Nation* cultural landscape perfectly. Songs that were raw and truthful and did not gloss over the awkward bits in life. Songs that spoke honestly of the messier aspects of romantic relationships and did not claim to be anything but embittered love songs. In short, a 19-year-old woman, newly introduced to the heartbreak club, spills her guts and, in doing so, finds that confessing her personal hurt and arranging it as great music makes her feel better.

"Being personal is my style," she told *The Independent* in 2004. "That's me. I'm never going to say things that other people have said in the same way. It wouldn't be interesting for me to hear it so it's not interesting for me to say it."

Meanwhile, Salaam Remi had come aboard the project and everybody was happy for him to produce Amy's album. When Stefan Skarbek heard that Amy was going to be flying out to Miami to work with Remi at his Creative Space studio, he knew it made sense.

"There are no regrets that I didn't continue working with her because I just generally feel that her path was different from mine and the tools that she needed to get what she has got, I didn't have; nor did Matt for that matter. She wanted someone who had those tools. Salaam Remi and Mark Ronson, they're not as bothered about the writing as they are about the Djing and the hip-hoppy stuff, which was always massively important to her. Mos Def she was mad about, always. But, really, she's a rock'n'roller who just happens to sing jazz. I think it was the right thing to do, to bring Salaam Remi in."

Remi, 31 at the time he got the call to join the project, grew up in New York City. His father, the musician and studio engineer, Van Gibbs, paved his son's path to the position of illustrious producer. Remi, who had his first drum kit at the age of three, got his first break playing keyboards for Kurtis Blow on the 1986 record, *Kingdom Blow*, which was produced by his father. He became fascinated with hip-hop and sampling. His father was often saying that he should *play* music, not sample it. This sent Remi back to study the recording and production techniques used on James Brown records. In the process, he also learned to play many instruments. He combined the three – studying those old James Brown recordings, a talent for various instruments, sampling – to arrive at his unique trademark style as producer and collaborator.

Remi then started building his own studio, sourcing rare and historically valuable equipment. With his unique approach and vintage equipment, he began to acquire a reputation on the hip-hop scene. He rocketed to mainstream attention when he produced The Fugees' 'Nappy Heads' and 'Fu-Gee-La' and Nas' hit single 'Made You Look' (which Amy loved). In tandem with this success, he became very interested in reggae, and branched out to work with various dancehall artists in the mid Nineties.

In 2002, in the aftermath of the 9/11 attacks, Remi made the decision to move his studio out of New York and down the West Coast to Miami, Florida. Down there, he was close to reggae musicians such as Troy Genius and Circle House Studios in Miami, which has mixed many classic Remi production jobs. It was then that he worked with Ms Dynamite.

Her cluster of heartbreak songs in hand, Amy flew out to Miami to meet Remi. Having been used to working in London with Skarbek and Rowe, she was suddenly in a different world. For a start, Remi had produced Nas, a rapper whose music she adored. Then, he had produced The Fugees' *The Score*, another album she rated very highly. His legendary studio, filled with a vast array of vintage as well as state-of-the-art musical equipment, spoke of creativity, artistic brilliance. As a producer, he was known for collaborating, shaping the music with the artist, honing their vision with his own unique approach to recording.

Island had decided to split the album and have Remi produce one body of material and another producer, Commissioner Gordon, work on another. This twin approach would prove successful and lead the label to repeat the formula for Amy's second album, *Back To Black*, which would be half produced by Salaam Remi and half by Mark Ronson. For the Remi half of *Frank*, Amy would record her tracks in Miami. For the Commissioner Gordon side of the album, she would fly up the East Coast and lay tracks at Gordon's home studio, The Headquarters, in New Jersey. They would also work on tracks in London (again at Mayfair Studios) and at Platinum Sound studios in New York.

Commissioner Gordon (aka Gordon Williams), in the capacity of producing, engineering and mixing records, had worked with the likes of KRS One, Will Smith, Whitney Houston and, notably, Lauryn Hill – he worked on her debut album *The Miseducation Of Lauryn Hill* – by the time he was placed on the *Frank* project. In short, Island was lining up heavyweights, and Darcus Beese must have had a clear vision for where he and the label thought Amy should have been heading. If Amy's goal was to be a jazz singer, Island was obviously envisaging setting her voice into more of an R&B/soul/hip-hop/reggae groove.

In Miami, Remi worked with Amy on getting the tracks sketched out, her vocals laid down. Mostly, this meant her playing guitar and singing. Once Amy had laid down her contributions and she and Remi had extensively discussed and tested arrangements and tempos, instruments and approaches, she left Miami. Remi then brought in a range of musicians to help him build the tracks up. One such musician was Jeni Fujita, a backing vocalist known for her work with Lauryn Hill and Wyclef Jean.

"My friend Salaam Remi called me and said, 'Come to Miami and lace up these backgrounds for me,'" recalls Fujita, from her home in Los Angeles. "So I came in and did all the backgrounds. I think some of Amy's lead was down but I think it might have just been a rough of her lead vocals. I didn't get to meet her. I came in and put the right vibe on it, like Salaam asked me to do."

Remi gave Fujita little instruction. He simply told her that when she heard the tracks, she'd know exactly what he was looking for. "Salaam pretty much just said, 'I'm working with this really powerful singer from the UK.' You hear her voice and he really didn't have to say much else, it was kind of like, hear, listen. 'Now go over there and do what you do.' It really is that simple when I'm working with someone like Salaam. He'd say, 'OK Jeni, go do what you do, I know it'll be good.' He gives direction when it's needed."

Fujita still remembers the first time Remi played her Amy's voice. "When I first heard her, I was like, 'Wait is that Lauryn (Hill)?' I really did hear a lot of Lauryn in there.' Not everybody agrees with me on that one but that's just how I heard it."

With Amy Winehouse being a new signing to Island, Fujita did not know much about the artist whose record she was singing on. "I didn't know who Amy was and I don't know that she knew she was going to be as big as she is. At that stage, when an artist is new, you just do your best, wish your best for these artists, because it's a tough business and I always put my good energy into any project and support that lead and wish the best for them."

Mostly, during the recording session, Remi let Fujita take the songs where she felt they should go. "Salaam trusted me to hear the vibe of the tracks; there were obviously jazz undertones and it was very soulful. Amy reminds me a lot of Lauryn Hill, so that was pretty easy for me to know what to do, to access the soul part of me and match what Amy had already put down and what Salaam had already included in the musical composition. It was pretty easy for me to figure out how to fit in there."

She then applied her characteristic talent for working with another voice, adding her soul to theirs. "One thing I've developed over time is how to support. As a back-up singer, it's about supporting, and I can't think of a better way of saying making them look better, just like adding the accent or the right colours to what they've already got. And if Lauryn or Amy have the deeper voice, I might add some highs. You have to give some different dimension to where they're at. If I'm singing with a really powerful singer, I won't sing really powerfully with them, I'll mould around them to bring them out more. I see it as like a piece of art where there are different colours, and there might be bolder colours or there might be accents that bring those bolder colours out."

With Amy being an emerging artist, the experience was very different from working with Lauryn Hill, as Fujita had on *The Miseducation of Lauryn Hill*. "With Lauryn, we were all together. She was giving us directions and she was in the studio producing things. She was really, really hands on. It was her first solo album. She had a lot more creative control. It was much more of a group. I was on tour with Wyclef Jean for almost a year and when Lauryn did *Miseducation*, she was really hands on. I'd get phone calls from her like, 'I need you to sing this high part because I can't hit the notes right now. Can you come in and do the highs?' And there were a group of us harmonising on 'Doo Wop (That Thing)'. It was a different experience from working on *Frank*, with Amy, a new artist. Salaam was much more in charge of things."

Another musician who Salaam Remi called upon was Troy Genius (aka Troy Wilson on the album liner notes), a Jamaican drummer turned Miami resident whose credits at the time included drumming for Redman, Bounty Killer and Dennis Brown.

"I was invited to the project by a close friend of mine Salaam Remi," remembers Genius, speaking from his home in Miami. "He was the one who was actually doing the project. We did Alicia Keys as well. Salaam's my very good friend and we work well together."

Remi asked Genius to come and add drums to the tracks he was working on. "I played on about four or five songs. He gave me all of his part of her album to play the drums for."

Like Jeni Fujita, Troy Genius was obviously not familiar with Amy Winehouse either. "I'd never heard of Amy before. Just like when Salaam and I were working on the Joss Stone album, I hadn't heard of her either until the album came out. So basically, it was just a project for me at first."

Genius was instrumental in helping Remi build the songs up from sketch form. They worked at Remi's studio, giving the songs rhythm, underpinning them with infectious beats. "When I got to the tracks," says Genius, "it was just her and the guitar, her sitting in and playing the guitar. And then we added everything that was needed on the tracks. I was working just with Salaam. I haven't met any of the other musicians. I just come in and do my part. Just like how we do any other project. He calls me up. I go down there. I do it with him. I don't live too far. I live in North Miami. It's about a 20-minute drive down the highway to Salaam's. There were a couple of songs that we wanted to make sure that it came out perfect. But it wasn't too hard because Salaam basically knew what he wanted and I just facilitated his production."

Like Fujita, Genius never met Amy either. She had already recorded, registered her magic, left it with Remi. As always, Remi brought his brilliance to the process. That's why so many of the songs are co-credited to Amy and Remi – he plays a genuinely intense creative role in the evolution of a body of music that blooms into an album.

"Salaam has a feel for the music," explains Genius. "He can duplicate anything that the client wants or the vibe that you portray to help the individual track. It was really fun to work on the album because of the different feel that we gave to it."

As when they had worked on music together before, Remi gave Genius a lovely sense of musical direction. "If you know Salaam you understand that he views music in texture. So he will tell me certain colours. You'd have to know him to really understand what I'm saying. But he sees it in colours and textures."

Mostly though, Genius' job was to give the songs a foundation. "I think I played a major part in constructing a groove or particular flavour for what she was singing about."

By the time his work on the tracks was done, Genius had a sense that the record would be successful. "To tell you the truth, ever since I met Salaam Remi, he doesn't do ordinary projects. Everything that he does comes out in the forefront, from The Fugees to Toni Braxton. We've done so much work, we played on *Rush Hour 3* the movie, the soundtrack for that. I anticipate that most if not all of his projects will be mainstream."

Meanwhile, on the other side of the record, Commissioner Gordon was working just as hard to bring his half of the material to the same standard. He too called on his own elite band of session musicians to help Amy lay down her tracks. One such musician was Earl Chinna Smith, the reggae guitarist known for his work with Bob Marley & The Wailers, Augustus Pablo, Black Uhuru, Burning Spear, Horace Andy, Prince Far I, Sizzla, Peter Tosh, King Tubby and Jimmy Cliff.

He and Gordon had worked together before. "I got a call from Commissioner Gordon," recalls Chinna Smith, talking from his home in Los Angeles. "He had come to Jamaica with Lauryn Hill and we did some stuff, like a couple of tracks. And a bass player, a friend of mine, Chris Meredith, who used to play with Ziggy Marley and Steve Marley, he came to Jamaica too and we did that stuff."

On *Frank*, Gordon wanted Smith to give Amy's tracks a Caribbean lilt. He had him fly out to meet Amy and the other musicians at his studio in New Jersey. "Amy came in and played guitar," says Chinna Smith of their first meeting. "And it was really fun and she smoke weed like we do. She got good energy."

Like everyone else working with Amy, Chinna Smith did not sense that the young singer was nervous in any way in the company of such experienced musicians. "She was very confident. I was impressed that she could play with our vibes. When I heard her sing, she sound to me like a young Sarah Vaughan, you know what I mean? Like those kinds of singers. I thought, wow. And she said she had some connection, a relative, I can't remember exactly, who was involved at this famous jazz club in England, Ronnie Scott's. So I know that she had this jazz background. So when she said that, I said woah man, you have that kind of musical background, now I know exactly why you sound like that."

A few hours into jamming and working on tracks, Chinna Smith was very impressed with Amy. "She came with so much talent and

Commissioner Gordon was really excited about it. She was singing so beautifully!"

They got into a groove, composing as they went, working with the same spontaneous elements that had fuelled her early songwriting sessions at Mayfair Studios with Skarbek and Rowe. "Our thing was you play the guitar, play some changes and then pile a beat and she writes. There were two songs like that she did."

In other cases, the tracks were complete, and all Gardner wanted Chinna Smith to do was record overdubs. Whether writing, recording or overdubbing, the days all had the same shape during the sessions. "We were staying at the producer's house. Amy'd come in like in the morning and she'd love to play, love to sing and we'd smoke weed. The herb is like a inspiration, a motivator."

By the second day, Chinna Smith's impressions of Amy had grown even warmer. "She was just this pure talented kid, so much love for music and wanting to get it out there."

Chinna Smith credits Gordon with creating a homely feel for the sessions, setting a familial atmosphere. "It was really beautiful," remembers the guitarist. "We were able to eat together. Amy like Thai food, I like Thai food too. I really enjoy doing that project."

During the sessions, as Amy sang her young Londoner's frank complaints of love gone wrong, Chinna Smith was struck by the freshness of what she had to say. "What really interests me in her lyrics is that they're a domestic revolutionary kind of thing, stuff people experience everyday. These lyrics and songs, they're something else. The attitude. It was unique of her to approach this stuff at that level. Wherever it come from, she's very clever."

When the sessions wrapped, Commissioner Gordon took his tracks and mixed them himself.

Salaam Remi, on the other hand, took his part of the record to Circle House Studios in Miami. He had already been recording the tracks with Gary "Mon" Noble from Circle House, so it was logical that Noble take the tracks and mix them to Remi's specifications.

Steve "ESP" Nowa was working with Noble and had been his assistant for some time. When he heard the tracks, he was so blown away that he talked Noble into letting him assist with the mixing. "I started working at Circle House Studios in 2001," recalls Nowa, now Head Engineer at the studio. "I was Head Assistant for quite some time and Salaam Remi was one of our best clients. I was assisting Gary Noble, working on every album that they did. And so when the Amy Winehouse project came in, her debut album, I was so excited when I heard the quality of the music that I asked Gary if I could help him mix. I actually wanted to get on the board and be part of it."

Once Noble agreed to co-mixing the tracks with Nowa, they got to work.

"We were in the studio every night mixing the songs down. We basically just stayed at the studio for weeks and months. Just tweaking these songs, getting them to sound the way they do. We spent a lot of time working on her vocals. The way that Salaam records, everything sounds really damn good as soon as you get it, because Salaam has more equipment than just about anybody in the United States. He has all the vintage gear. So everything he records basically sounds good. And so we were like putting final touches on everything."

Nowa says that Remi offered gentle direction, but mostly trusted them, as he trusted Jeni Fujita, to take the tracks where they needed to go.

"Salaam is a very technical person, so when he's speaking with people that speak the language of music, he's gonna speak in a different way. But when he speaks to us, he's very technical, because he can mix a song himself. Salaam knows how to run all the equipment that we use. It's more technical. Salaam can walk in a room and tell you exactly what frequency he needs boosted or cut. And Gary has worked with him for so long that Gary basically knows what he's looking for."

If Remi did offer input or direction, it was in a general, oblique way, for instance giving them music that had a particular sound or element he wanted them to use as a moodboard. "Salaam would come to the studio and sometimes he'd leave us a stack of CDs and he would be, like, 'Listen to this instrument on this CD and this instrument on this CD'. He'd tell us certain things that he liked about certain songs and he would ask us to listen to those references and try to incorporate all of those small details into his records."

From the first time he heard Amy's voice and twisted Noble's arm into letting him assist with the mixing, Nowa was struck by the power of her voice.

"Amy's vocals are out of this world. Her tone just sounds vintage. Basically, we were just messing around blending a bunch of different effects to make her vocal like a perfect, warm, clear cloud that just ran the track but had some mystery and that vintage tone to it."

Much of their work involved piecing together the best elements and takes, polishing Remi's already potent work. "A lot of times we'd go through a lot of different takes with the musicians and we'd kinda just pick stuff that worked with the ad libs that she'd be singing at the time. And we'd kinda just beef everything together. But when it was mixing time, it was just mixing time. We were alone and we just had free range to do what we wanted to do."

Nowa soon had a clear sense of what made the tracks tick, take off, ignite.

"It was the combination of Amy's vocal and the tracks that Salaam was making."

When he and Noble were almost finished with the mixing, executives came to check out the work. "The label came at the end. Basically they didn't really have a lot of problems. They just wanted to sit down and go over all the final mixes with us. But there really weren't many big details from the label. If we had something small, we had to go do a recall."

When they were officially done, Nowa knew it was an important record. "I felt from the first moment I heard it that it was gonna be a huge success. Because I figured that if they had the type of budget that they were here working on with us and Salaam was doing production, then they had budget enough to push it correctly. And I just knew as soon as I heard the songs that it sounded like something the world needed. Because it sounded like great music."

Chapter Four

Frank

Despite some reported minor tussles with Island about the selection of one or two mixes for the album, Amy and the label finally smoothed out the running order for the album and *Frank* was finished. The cover for the album, shot by Charles Moriarty, showed a wholesome, smiling, tanned Amy Winehouse walking a cute little black dog – a whole lifetime away, in terms of image, from the Amy Winehouse of *Back To Black*, with her dozen or so tattoos and dramatically skinny physique. In a pink off-the-shoulder top, she looks like any regular 19-year-old young woman of the time, as if snapped taking her pet dog for a quick walk around the block. It's an image that somehow doesn't fit the content of the album, especially when juxtaposed with the "parental advisory explicit content" sticker slapped on the front, on account of the record's healthy use of expletives. Considering how Island was bringing in the likes of Salaam Remi and Commissioner Gordon, it's surprising that the album cover doesn't make more of a play for Amy's black-sounding voice, her African-American inspired music, the broad American roots of her musical leanings. Instead, it's a nice, homely sort of shot, somewhere between Carole King on the cover of her mullti-million selling album *Tapestry*, and Norah Jones on the cover of her multi-million selling debut album *Come Away With Me*.

The other photographs, by Valerie Phillips, show a more real, everyday, intimate Amy – before a mirror putting on make-up getting ready to go out, playing pool (one of Amy's favourite pastimes apparently), getting ready to smoke a joint, checking in her handbag for something while out, a shot of what is presumably her CD collection, a shot of accessories (bangles and a shoe) – and flesh out the plot basics of some of the album's songs, in which a young woman in London tells the story of a failed relationship with a man seven years her senior. The photograph of the CD collection is particularly fascinating, as it gives clear insights into what Amy wanted listeners to know she had been listening to on the short life journey that led to the creation of this album: Thelonius Monk, the *Rocky Horror Picture Show* soundtrack, TLC, Beck, Wu-Tang Clan, Busta Rhymes, Michael Jackson, Miles Davis, Rage Against The Machine, Talib Kweli, Frank Sinatra, The Roots, De La Soul, Ella Fitzgerald, Mahalia Jackson, Red Hot Chili Peppers, Sheryl Crow and so on. Many of the album titles are out of focus, but, of what you can see, there are some real surprises, particularly Sheryl Crow.

Frank does not begin like the debut album by a new pop sensation. It strolls into play with a little skit, 'Stronger Than Me (Intro)'. A bassist and guitarist both walk busily around their fretboards while, over the top, there's a woman scat singing. It's smoochy, midnight hour, lived in. It does not sound like a vocal laid down by a 19-year-old. There's age to the voice, more like the vocal improvisation of a seasoned jazz veteran, a woman who's perhaps sung at every jazz club from one side of North America to the other. The intention, for sure, is that this debut recording by a young female artist launches her on a jazz trip. There are to be no mistakes with labelling or genre-tags. This young woman considers herself a jazz singer, from the tip of the skull to the point of her toes. The vocal, in its style, references the great lineage of female jazz singers before her and, second to that, in its spirit, the great lineage of female blues singers before her. The voice is timeless, knows its roots, its sense of history. There's a knowingness to the channels the music comes from. They're old, as old as the singer is young. And in that discrepancy, for everyone else: fascination.

The opening of the record defies the simple tagging of a sound. It's not a now sound, for sure. It's not the new sound. It's not an artist turning popular music on its head, reinventing. This is not Elvis Presley releasing 'That's All Right (Mama)' or The Beach Boys releasing *Pet Sounds* or The Beatles releasing *Sgt Pepper's Lonely Hearts Club Band* or My Bloody Valentine releasing *Glider*. This is a 19-year-old woman singing the ghosts of jazz in 2003. The key detail, though, is that those twenty seconds of 'Stronger Than Me' (Intro) do not sound like 2003.

But then the beat kicks in. A soulful shuffle that wouldn't sound out of place on Lauryn Hill's *The Miseducation Of Lauryn Hill* or Macy Gray's *On How Life Is* or Eryka Badu's *Baduizm*. The polished, jazzy guitar licks cruise smoothly over the beat, beneath her voice. Huffs of sax, smooches of Sixties pump organ, add further shading. The bass bulges in, here, there, observing distant reggae grooves. And then, over the top, the voice. A soul singer, a jazz singer, a blues singer, an R&B singer. The vocal is thrilling. Checks Billie Holiday, Macy Gray, Lauryn Hill, Neneh Cherry, Mary J Blige. And then there's the lyric – a firm, assertive complaint to a boyfriend; disgruntled notes on a relationship not quite satisfying. The line of thought is a woman's grumble: the boyfriend isn't masculine enough, isn't acting his role – that of the man – to a sufficient degree. She feels the pressure of carrying elements of his traditional gender role in their relationship. Her complaint turns harsh, becomes a lover's sting, a barbed remark: she asks the boyfriend if he's gay. She wants a man in her life, not a considerate, touchy feely "new man" happy to blur gender roles and stereotypes in a relationship.

These relationship politics come to the song forcefully but as a narrative. This is not the harsh put-down of, say a Missy Elliott song (compare 'Stronger Than Me' with Elliott's 'One Minute Man'), nor the explicit, groaning slapdown of a Lil' Kim track. Instead, it's a strong woman who wants a man who can stand shoulder to shoulder, at the bare minimum, ideally usurp her at times, offer a challenge, keep her keen. Similar relationship politics graced Liz Phair's 1993 album, *Exile In Guyville*, her song-for-song riposte to the Rolling Stones' 1972 album, *Exile On Main Street*. Phair's radical album, which saw her complaining about typical male traits in a woman's pursuit of love, featured tracks like 'Fuck And Run', about men sweet-talking women into a one-night stand and then fleeing in the morning, without so much as a goodbye.

Winehouse arrived at this album with a similarly strong feeling about what she wanted to say. Her subject was to be relationship politics. And her angle was that of a strong minded, no-nonsense, post-feminist 19-year-old North London girl who had been dumped by her boyfriend. She brought to her Lauryn Hill-meets-Billie Holiday songs the opinions of a young woman weaned on a TV show like *Sex And The City*. This was a young woman who knew what she did and didn't like in a man and was quite happy to write candidly about her experiences and disappointments, regardless of whose ego (the ex-boyfriend's obviously) got scuffed along the way.

The song was not as simple however as a strong woman wanting an equally strong or stronger man. It was about a woman who craved old-school masculinity – personified by actors like James Dean, Robert De Niro, Marlon Brando and Matt Dillon. It was a song about a woman who definitely wasn't going to play second fiddle to her boyfriend but who, conversely, wanted her boyfriend to take the lead. A fascinating fusing of feminist ideals and traditionalism. Hence the album's title. The songs were both the frank musings of a 19-year-old woman and a homage to the kind of man Frank Sinatra was: macho, tough, traditional. A man, in other words, arguably not unlike Amy's father, Mitch.

Track three, 'You Send Me Flying', opens like an Eartha Kitt song from the Seventies, the glitterball of piano chords a call to the dance floor. The voice – somewhere between Kitt, Diana Ross, Sade and Donna Summer – again climbs above the music, flies passionately. You catch the first lyric – a woman singing about lending a boyfriend two albums: a record by the Outsidaz and the new record by Erykah Badu – and suddenly it's bang up to date. After the jazzy red herring of the intro, the album's now moving into a clearer, more urban sound, bringing together Amy's interests in jazz, blues, R&B, hip-hop and soul music. This contemporary love story moves on with references to the boyfriend's Beastie Boys records. Throughout, the exquisite, clean, clipped electric guitar, flicking off laid-back licks. When the chorus climbs up, rides that loping drum track, it sounds like Soul II Soul in their prime. Near the end, the vocal ad libs, riffing on notions of injured pride, soar, almost pull the music to torch song status.

The drumbeat that opens 'Know You Now' carries along bird calls, a Caribbean lilt. The song sounds like a vintage Seventies soul tune. Here is the black R&B feel, underpinned with jazzy musings, referencing Alicia Keys, Erykah Badu, Macy Gray, Eartha Kitt, Lauryn Hill. Her voice switches in and out of reminding the listener of Billie Holiday and Lauryn Hill. In any case, it's one of those tracks on the album in which it's particularly hard to process that the woman singing is young, white, Jewish and British – four tags that contradict the voice burning off the groove.

'Fuck Me Pumps', with its dancehall flavour and driving Lauryn Hill drumbeat, is a mischievous survey of a certain kind of woman on a quest for Mr Right. Amy satirically runs down a checklist of the personality traits of such a woman – aspiring to bag a tall, handsome, rich man who can commit and give her the fabled life of the footballer's wife – while chronicling her sad life of one-night stands, mishaps and dashed hopes, all the while caked in makeup, high heels, skin-tight jeans and the latest designer clothes. Amy sharpens her claws here, let's rip with a *Sex And The City* meets *Cosmopolitan* assassination of what she sees as the most fickle and brittle example of her fellow gender. Near the end, the doo-wop backing vocals offer a tiny signpost of where her music will go when she sets out to write and record her second album, *Back To Black*. She explained to *The Times* in 2004 who the song was aimed at: "Some women think they're validated by a wedding ring or having a rich boyfriend. But they're not things you should strive for. So it's about those kinds of girls. But there's so many bitches out there, I can't take it."

From there Amy switches to a delicious, laid-back, jazzy groove with 'I Heard Love Is Blind'. The guitar, flute, shuffling drums and prods of bass back her up, support this showcase of her remarkable vocals. Another love-done-me-wrong song, clocking in at a mere two minutes, it has a spontaneous, heartbroken feel. The lyric seems raw, tossed off, a singer looking to cleanse her heartache on the spot rather than let it fester. It's Amy Winehouse doing what Amy Winehouse does best: channelling the immediacy of a present-tense upset and crisis into great music. Acting on the spot, blasting a private diary or journal entry if you will, across fine music. It's her candid turn of phrase that pulls her female take on romance away from pop music's cliched renderings of love as the ultimate battlefield. This is different. It's not whiny or pining. It's not soft or passive. These are songs that aggressively state the opinions of a young woman on the lookout for love and fun in London in the early days of the 21st century.

Track six, 'Moody's Mood For Love', a sunny reggae/dancehall cut, bears all the hallmarks of Earl Chinna Smith's fine reggae licks and the busy reggae bass playing of Salaam Remi himself. A cover of the jazz standard, popularised by King Pleasure's version in 1952, the mood is laidback, an echo on the drum track referencing classic dub records. Amy's voice weaves around exquisite backing vocals from Jeni Fujita and improvises wonderfully, squeezing double-length lines. The song fades out, dropping into a cocktail jazz groove, warm sax.

'(There Is) No Greater Love' begins like Billie Holiday dragged to the year 2003. A cover of the 1936 jazz standard by composer/bandleader Isham Jones and Marty Symes, it has crickets chirping, flute, understated bass, piano, chiming guitar. A midnight mood, for sure, with Amy crooning over the top, like she's got one foot in Forties New York and the other in 2003 Jamaica. The song is a sketch, like 'Moody's Mood For Love', the production team respecting Amy's knack for spontaneous excellence. The song also cleverly references the Norah Jones/Jamie Cullum vibe of the time, while strongly pitching its sound and content to fans of black American music.

Then in stomp the beats of 'In My Bed', which references the trip-hop sounds of Portishead/Tricky as well as the pulsating apocalyptic hip-hop magic of Wu-Tang Clan. Vocally, the jazz side of Amy Winehouse is on hold, while to the fore is the Amy Winehouse who appreciates the music of Lauryn Hill and Erykah Badu. The Seventies soul references of the choir-like backing vocals and wailing flute build on the thumping bass/drumbeat and the kind of reggae guitar touches that you typically hear on a Massive Attack record. The lyric appears to be another relationship wars story – this time it's the scathing warning of a woman to her ex-lover that while they might have fallen into bed yet again, it doesn't mean that the relationship's back on. It was just fun, old comforts, easy because both know it's easy, even if in the morning it'll be the same old mess again.

Track nine, 'Take The Box', is the album's standout love song; a classic break-up track, all about packing up and sending a lover on his way. It's the closest song to pop on the album – some of the backing vocals for instance wouldn't sound out of place on an All Saints single. The lyric is another Amy Winehouse story as song lyric – told/sung as truthfully as possible: complete with contemporary commentary, expletives and slang. It's a break-up story as if told as a North Londoner's answer to *Sex And The City*. As with so many tracks on the album, it showcases the remarkable emotional registers that her voice is capable of reaching.

'October Song', another track that begins with a Lauryn Hill-esque Caribbean/soul/R&B groove, tells the story of the death of Amy's pet canary. Her voice soars across the track, reminiscent of Macy Gray and the Billie Holiday-influenced American R&B artist, Lina. A metaphorical song that bumps along colourfully, Amy's voice again soars across the band, reminding listeners that this album is about the voice, the vocal delivery, the vocal style, a singer's record above all else.

The turntable scramble at the start of 'What Is It About Men' announces the band's stepping into a Seventies Lenny Kravitz/ Lauryn Hill groove. There are flavours of the Rolling Stones ('Fool To Cry'), Bob Marley (try playing 'I Shot The Sheriff' at half speed and enjoy the loose comparison between that classic and 'What Is It About Men'), The Afghan Whigs (in the merging of white rock/ black soul) and Macy Gray's guitar-slammed modern R&B sounds.

One of the most infectious tracks on the album, the horn-led summertime love letter of 'Help Yourself', opens with reggae rhythms, shimmering maracas, plucked acoustic guitars, lumbering bass, the thud of the snare drum, letting Amy speak directly to her lover. The horns reference big-band jazz while Amy dishes another complaint to a lover. Despite its love in a tailspin subject, the song, a lover telling a 25-year-old partner to sort his act out, is incredibly upbeat, positive. It's a song that literally skips to its end, casually pursuing a lazy beat with the laid-back cool you typically associate with a soul-flavoured Lou Reed song.

The album's closing track, 'Amy Amy Amy', comes galloping into play like a Tom Waits song on the prowl or playful cabaret. The double bass struts, the drums drunkenly embellish the rhythm, while Amy drawls her story, chased by trumpet. It's a smoky, seductive Billie Holiday/Nina Simone song, riffing on desire, the lyric and groove very loosely suggesting allusions to 'Fever'. While it might sound like a gin-soaked Thirties stomp in a New York jazz club, the lyrics once more speak of a young London-based woman's contemporary love life, as references to her object of attraction wearing Diesel jeans pin the song firmly to modern times.

The album plays out with 'Amy Amy Amy (Outro)', a cut of improvised jazz, cruising across the rubble of 'Amy Amy Amy'. The MC signs off the album as if the listener's been locked to a live performance by a jazz/soul diva. Seconds of dead time pass and then 'Amy Amy Amy (Outro)' drifts into a soul/jazz mood, underpinned by what sounds like a drum machine. It's got the mark of Sade, a smooth-midnight blue sound. When that drifts out, in comes another classic soul-inspired beat, Amy singing over horns, crisp guitar. The album unofficially plays out to hidden track 'Mr Magic', soaring horns rising to a peak.

Chapter Five

Made You Look

That summer, while Remi and Gordon worked their magic on her debut album, Amy had been finding her voice live. Paul Franklin at Helter Skelter, the booking agency division of the Sanctuary group, had made an approach to Christian Barnes of 4stickslive and arranged for Amy to perform a trio of dates at the Cobden on Kensal Road, West London. Barnes, a promoter, listened to Amy's demo and scheduled her first show at the Cobden for July 22, 2003. She appeared solo, just her and her guitar, as at the pub gigs of the previous year. The night she appeared was specifically geared to emerging acts.

"The night I promote," says Barnes, "is not exactly an open mic, but more a footing for up and coming acts and those at a higher level who are about to be picked up. Such names have included Tom Baxter, KT Tunstall, Anna Krantz, Duke Special and Ben's Brother, and the genres are very eclectic but I do try to match as best I can. Punk and hard rock don't play."

A month later, on August 11, Amy played again at the Cobden, this time with a full band. Things were changing fast, her sound developing and enlarging as she began to conceive taking *Frank* out on the road. Considering she was playing a night geared to emerging artists and bands, did Barnes remember her standing out as one of those who would make it?

"We've seen thousands of artistes at the Cobden over the last four years. To remember an individual performer they must be special. Amy's in that category. She was very shy and didn't have much to say for herself but, when she sang with her now trademark vocal, something special happened in the room. She didn't have the hits like 'Rehab' back then but she always had the voice."

The third in her trio of gigs was on September 1, 2003, six weeks or so shy of *Frank* being released. This time, it was her and her guitar accompanied by a keyboard player. By this show, there was a buzz. Barnes, who was unaware that Amy was signed to Island when Franklin approached him, certainly knew by this point that things were happening for the young singer.

"If she learned anything from playing at the Cobden it was how to draw people in simply by using her voice," says Barnes. "I didn't know about her deals at the time and wouldn't have expected her to be a pop star, but soon after this show at the Cobden, the posters for *Frank* started to appear. That put her performances at the club into perspective. The gigs were her last as an anonymous performer and, thinking back, we were indeed watching her blossom into the live performer we see now."

In the audience, about to become a fan, was Annie Lennox. "By pure coincidence," Barnes recalls, "Annie Lennox came to the club on the night of Amy's last gig with us. She was recording at the time in a studio down the road and was checking out the venue."

Lennox told *The Times* in 2007 what she made of the young artist's performance that night. "I was completely blown away," said the former Eurythmics singer. "She was like a woman in her thirties, with a whole, seasoned delivery, not fazed by anything at all. I was in awe of her. I thought, wow, you have a special talent. God, you are 18, where did that come from?"

And then it was October and time for Amy's debut recordings to be released to record shops. On October 6, Island issued Amy's first single, 'Stronger Than Me', backed with 'What It Is', a cut not on the album, while a remix of 'Take The Box' was added as a bonus track.

The cover of the single, as with the album, portrayed Amy in a fairly nondescript fashion, sitting, her long hair falling over her shoulders, wearing a pink vest and brightly coloured Hawaiian-style summer skirt. The look was natural, the emphasis on Amy as real and easy to relate to, an image designed to reflect the unfussy, what-you-see-is-what-you-get element of the single's lyric.

Pushed hard by the label, 'Stronger Than Me' won a round of positive reviews from intrigued critics, but despite this it didn't sell especially fast or well, and ended up peaking at number 71 on the UK singles chart.

The album, *Frank*, followed two weeks later, and launched Amy into a British music scene preoccupied with a so-called youthful jazz revival or New Jazz scene. On account of her love of jazz and the album's jazzy inclinations, Amy found herself pitched on to this bandwagon and lumped in with Jamie Cullum, Katie Melua (who also attended the BRIT school) and Norah Jones, all now darlings of the successful new easy-listening-jazz-meets-pop hybrid.

The sonic landscape of *Frank* – warm, jazzy, laid-back, but with a distinct urban sound – actually set her apart from Cullum, Melua and Jones. At that time, however, with her declarations of love for old-school jazz legends like Ella Fitzgerald, Billie Holiday and Sarah Vaughan coursing through every interview, critics all too eagerly included her in the same category as this trio of evolving singers, all of whom, especially Jones, had achieved some measure of success. There were definite parallels though, even if Amy's lyrics on *Frank* were grittier and suggested dirty fingernails and smeared lipstick traces.

After the success of his 2002 debut album, *Pointless Nostalgic*, and healthy word-of-mouth hype for his live shows, Jamie Cullum found himself thrust into the spotlight when he was signed to Universal Classics & Jazz. His second album, *Twentysomething*, characterised by his soft crooning, retro jazz style married to poppy, jazzy easy listening tunes, was released on October 20 2003, the same day as *Frank*, and soon became a massive hit.

It was probably intentional that *Frank* and *Twentysomething* were released on the same day. Amy and Cullum were two young artists –

one 19, the other 24 – both infatuated with jazz, both British and both also interested in blues, hip-hop, soul and R&B. It was inevitable that reviewers would lump them together, and in this way the publicity department at Island had ensured that at the very least Amy's debut wouldn't be ignored.

The Daily Telegraph ran a feature that month looking at Cullum's sure-to-be-successful album, and within it considered how he and Amy fit the new jazz mood. Cullum told the paper: "What I'm doing isn't pure jazz. I don't really make distinctions between genres, which is something you get from dance music, where everything gets thrown into the mix. I grew up with pop, rock, indie, dance, hip-hop, and the thing that fascinated me about jazz was that you can kind of mould all these influences into one." The report also checked Norah Jones and Amy Winehouse: "The global success of Norah Jones has put crossover jazz back on the music-business radar. Universal's other major British signing this year, Amy Winehouse, also offers a contemporary spin on jazz and soul."

Norah Jones, meanwhile, had arrived first. Her hugely successful debut album, *Come Away With Me*, had been released in February 2002 by Blue Note, a classy label with a long tradition of excellence in the jazz field. The album pitched Jones as a jazzy, soul-flavoured easy-listening pop diva, her piano-led music a slightly more soulful take on the intimate textures of Carole King's multi-million selling 1971 album, *Tapestry*. Jones was the eye-catching daughter of Indian sitar legend Ravi Shankar, and media coverage about her background ensured she got a head start on Cullum and Amy. They had much in common though, not least a liking for Billie Holiday, a key influence on Jones' sultry, soulful vocal style.

For the most part, *Frank* was very well received. *The Guardian*, for instance, said of her debut, "Winehouse sounds as if she has performed a thousand times in smoky jazz clubs. Sitting something between Nina Simone and Erykah Badu, Winehouse's sound is at once innocent and sleazy." The review highlighted 'Take The Box' as the "standout track" on the album, describing it as a "stunningly soulful tale of returning an ex-lover's possessions". *The Times'* review stated, "Winehouse has channelled an adolescence immersed in jazz, soul and hip-hop into a beguiling hybrid that, in the debts it owes, drops all the right musical names of yesteryear, but simultaneously manages to sound thrillingly new. No wonder Island pricked up its ears." *The Daily Telegraph* said, "North Londoner Winehouse is 19, writes like Cole Porter, sings like Billie Holiday, plays snooker like a pro."

In its review, *The Jewish Chronicle* zoomed in on the artist's youthfulness, introducing the album as being "astonishingly accomplished" for a debut by someone so young. The reviewer checked that Winehouse had been labelled a "feisty loose tongued Jewish teenager from Camden", but went on to say that in his opinion, the album sounded "more as if she were a feisty Jewish teenager from the Bronx, steeped in the Sarah Vaughan back catalogue". He highlighted her "smoky vocal style and word lyrics", pointing out how they fronted songs that flitted between "late night jazz and looping lazy beats – it's not for nothing that she namechecks Dinah Washington and the Beastie Boys on the album sleeve". Like other critics assessing the album, he saw the dangers of it acquiring a late-night jazz tag, placing Winehouse in the same camp as a singer like Sade, but concluded that with songs like 'Fuck Me Pumps', this was somewhat unlikely.

Mere weeks after *Twentysomething* and *Frank* came the debut album by another 19-year-old female singer with similar smooth, jazzy pop leanings: Katie Melua. Melua had first sprung to attention during the summer of 2003 with her debut single, 'The Closest Thing To Crazy', which was picked up by BBC Radio 2 and became a Top 10 hit. Like Winehouse, Melua had attended the BRIT School for the Performing Arts and Technology. Her debut album, *Call Off The Search*, was produced (and partly written) by Mike Batt and released independently on his Dramatico label on November 3, just two weeks after *Frank* and Cullum's debut. *Call Off The Search* took off quickly and hit number one on the album chart in January 2004. Always keen to attach labels, critics had by then identified a new movement that they termed "pop jazz", because records so catagorised were selling fast to British record buyers.

Melua later reflected on this so-called movement in an interview with music OMH.com, saying, "People like me and Jamie and Norah

(Jones) and Amy Winehouse – it's sad to say – but people like us have always been around but the timing was right for us to go into the mainstream because that's what the public wanted and needed."

On Halloween, 2003, *The Jewish Chronicle* ran a story on Amy. It was logical, with her being a north London Jewish girl and *The Jewish Chronicle*, know affectionately as the *JC* to readers, devoted in its arts focus to covering the work of Jewish artists. The journalist introduced her as follows: "If you saw her in synagogue, you'd think Amy Winehouse was your average north London Jewish girl especially since she was brought up in a close-knit, middle-class family, but you'd be wrong." The piece focused on her age, 20, honing in on the precocious position the "feisty songstress" was in. Asked how she'd best describe the sound of *Frank*, Amy said, "My sound is very jazz based, with a hip hop and R&B influence. I sound like one of those old jazz singers." She told the paper her musical idols were Madonna and Grace Jones, Madonna because "she's not afraid to express herself sexually", and Jones because "she didn't care". Of her songs, she said they were personal in inspiration and predominantly "about relationships with men. I've got a sharp tongue but there's humour in there as well. Also, I may be knocking my boyfriend, but I knock myself as well".

In support of the album, Amy was out there, promoting the record live, putting the practice of the Cobden shows into play. Mostly, despite some solo dates, she was supporting Jamie Cullum – a billing that served only to fan the "new jazz" hysteria and further pigeonhole Amy as a contemporary of Norah Jones and her tour mate. After those dates, on November 13, she opened for Finley Quaye at the Shepherd's Bush Empire. music OHM.com was there and reviewed the show, saying: "Amy Winehouse's performance was let down by poor sound. The promising youngster evidently has a powerful voice but it came across as harsh-sounding at this gig. She achieved a more pleasant tone when she was singing low-key numbers rather than the belters. Both her material, which was a blend of jazz, pop and funk with a splash of reggae, and her voice, were reminiscent of a jazz Nelly Furtado. However, her brass section could go a little easier on the predictable sax solos."

On November 24, yet another female artist with a powerful blues voice that belied her age released her debut album. Indeed, Joss Stone was only 16 at the time of *The Soul Sessions*, a mere fledgling compared to Amy. On Stone's second album, *Mind Body & Soul*, she would also work with Commissioner Gordon and Salaam Remi, the producers behind Amy's *Frank*. Overnight, Stone, Winehouse and Melua were grouped together as three incredibly young female British singers whose music bestowed a thrilling maturity.

Tellingly, as *Frank* took off in the UK and 2003 came to a close, there were still no plans to release it in the US. Island had presumably decided it was best to begin at home, see how the record sold domestically before making the big leap into the increasingly complex and often bizarre American market. Despite the Gordon/Remi production and the album's strong referencing of American jazz and blues, married to an obvious urban contemporary sound, the label was curiously reluctant to invest in trying to break Amy across the Atlantic at this stage in her career.

Back home, Amy found herself having to fend off claims that she was pop svengali Simon Fuller's latest creation. After all, it was Fuller who had unleashed The Spice Girls on an unsuspecting world and followed up with S Club 7, a septet whose music was hardly a benchmark for integrity. Amy was strong in defending herself though, and dismissed her associations with Fuller's pop stable. Later, in 2007, she explained to *The Sunday Tribune* that her relationship with Fuller was tenuous, to say the least. "It's important I get this right," she said. "I was managed by a guy called Nick Godwin who was funded by Simon Fuller. I've literally met (Fuller) once. As soon as my contract was up I ran away."

On December 5, Amy took to the stage at Bush Hall, a fairly intimate venue with a capacity of just 350 on Uxbridge Road in west London's Shepherd's Bush. It was her first major London showcase as a headlining act and a step up from playing the Cobden, which has a maximum capacity of 300. Her band included a drummer, a three-piece brass section, two guitarists (one switched back and forth between guitar and keyboards) and a bassist. She herself played electric and acoustic guitar. On account of all the hype surrounding

Frank, reporters from the British broadsheets were in attendance. *The Guardian's* review mused, "Her first substantial London headline show pinged around confusedly for a while – Winehouse and her brass section jostled for space on the pocket-sized stage, and when at one point they wandered off, she hissed, Come on!" The review did, however, end on a positive note, saying, "Winehouse is the very definition of potential. She's got some way to go before she matches Erykah Badu, to whom she's frequently compared, for emotion and technique, but long may her angst unfurl." *The Times* was also there, but its reviewer wasn't convinced by the live show, noting, "Some of the late-night sleaziness of *Frank* was absent, perhaps because Winehouse was nervous, or maybe because it was hard to hear her bitchiest lyrics – the singer's put-downs of men are a priceless part of her album."

Despite the interest in the new jazz-inspired fad of the year, only Norah Jones made the top-selling UK albums list of 2003, along with Dido's *Life For Rent*, Justin Timberlake's *Justified*, Christina Aguilera's *Stripped* and Daniel Bedingfield's *Gotta Get Thru This*. Although *Frank* would eventually reach number 13 on the chart, that peak did not occur in 2003. Sales failed to ignite even though the album attracted several warm reviews, all of which focused on Amy as a strong-minded artist with a startling voice and a way with a tough, gritty lyric. This was probably because *Frank* wasn't an easy listen like Norah Jones' debut album, like Jamie Cullum's second album or like Katie Melua's debut. All these were the sort of record that could be played softly in the background, as an accompaniment to dinner parties at which they were unlikely to intrude on polite conversation. *Frank*, on the other hand, was a much bolder proposition, a musically eclectic blend of jazz, blues, soul, reggae and hip-hop, and its lyrics were earthy, no-nonsense statements, especially in the case of 'Fuck Me Pumps'. It was difficult to imagine Norah Jones or Katie Melua uttering such an obscenity, which, in the case of *Frank*, meant the CD case was adorned with a parental advisory sticker. The songs themselves, while certainly memorable, contain none of the catchy pop choruses that would characterise it as a Simon Fuller creation. Indeed, *Frank* is at times difficult listening, so it was never going to be an easy sell for Island, and this is probably why the label held back on pushing it at

the American market. With too many rough edges, too many uncom-
promising chord changes and too many pungent lyrics, the album
was unlikely to break American radio in the way that Norah Jones
could expect to do. So, as 2003 gave way to 2004, Amy could bask in
the critical reaction that *Frank* had received even if there was a long
way to go. She was getting written up, but middle England really had
no idea who she was.

★ ★ ★

At the turn of 2004, Amy decided she'd had enough of being lumped
in with the new-jazz movement and set about declaring herself independent of it. In an interview with music OMH.com, she launched a
scathing attack on those who'd compared her with Jamie Cullum,
Norah Jones and Katie Melua. "People put us together because we
have come out at the same time, but we're nothing alike. I feel bad for
Jamie being lumped in with me and her (Melua). I'm a songwriter
and she has her songs written for her. He must feel frustrated. She
must think it's her fucking lucky day. If anyone stands out straight
from us, it would be her. Because she doesn't write her own songs. It's
not like she's singing old songs like Jamie, she's singing shit new songs
that her manager writes for her."

The bravado cheered off the release of the second single from
Frank, 'Take The Box', which Island released on January 12, 2004.
With another bland cover, a profile shot of Amy from the bust up, tar-
geting her at an indiscriminate pop audience, it was clear the label
was still unsure how to market her. Faring better than 'Stronger Than
Me', 'Take The Box' peaked at number 57 on the UK singles chart.
Backed with ''Round Midnight' and a live version of 'Stronger Than
Me', the record, while still not the hit Island must have been hoping
for, nevertheless indicated an upswing in Amy's fortunes.

On January 23, *The Jewish Chronicle* ran a piece highlighting Amy's
rapid rise to fame, hooking it on the forthcoming BRIT awards ceremony, which was scheduled to be held on February 17. The piece,
unlike the Halloween profile, caught the wind of the Amy Winehouse
success story, stating, "Isn't she known for being a bit gorgeous?" and

then went on to pronounce her a "foul mouthed tattoooed rock chick with attitude".

In February, *The Independent* ran a Q&A with Amy. Asked about her twin nominations for two BRIT awards (Best urban act/Best British female solo artist), her answer turned into a stinging attack on the fast-route-to-fame conceit that was a consequence of the immense popularity of the TV show *Pop Idol*, which was launched in 2001. "I never wanted any of this and that's the truth," she said. "I would have been happy to sing in a covers band for the rest of my life. And I wouldn't have gone on one of those shows in a million, billion years, because I think that musicality is not something other people should judge you on. Music's a thing you have with yourself." She also expressed her wariness of the music industry publicity machine, declaring, "I've given them a lot of control. I made the music because I know how to do that, but then for the promotional side I stepped back and thought, 'I've got to trust this lot', because I've never done this before. That was the wrongest thing I could have done. All they know how to do is what's already been done and I don't want to do anything that's already been done. I don't ever want to do anything mediocre. Learning from music is like eating a meal. You have to pace yourself. You can't take everything from it all at once. I want to be different, definitely. I'm not a one-trick pony. I'm at least a five-trick pony."

That interview with *The Independent* heralded the full emergence of Amy Winehouse as an opinionated interviewee. In an era when bland, self-serving interviews were the order of the day, when publicists demanded written notification of all questions likely to be posed in interviews, and were likely to remove their client from the arena if the questions veered off the agenda, this was a refreshing blast of reality. From here on in, Amy fully spoke her mind, just like she should, being the daughter of sharp-witted parents. She did not mince words or hold back on opinions. If she thought something, she said it, regardless of how many feathers got ruffled. This directness would become part of her trademark – a strong woman with a big voice and plenty to say.

On March 5 and 6, Amy played two dates at the Pizza Express jazz club in London's Soho. She did not sing with her usual band but instead performed with The Bradley Webb Trio. Abandoning her usual guitar accompaniment, she sang a mix of her own songs and a smattering of covers. Amy's father, Mitch, took to the stage at one point, handling vocal duties for a Frank Sinatra cover. According to *The Telegraph*'s review, "Mitch seemed unimpressed by some of the trio's experimental trimmings. With all the casual menace of an *EastEnders* villain, he paused his performance to inquire of the fresh faced piano player, 'Was that the bridge or are you just doodling about as usual?'"

★ ★ ★

It was nearly spring and Amy's favourite record of the moment was Outkast's *Speakerboxx/The Love Below*. The double album featured a solo album apiece from each half of the Atlanta hip-hip duo. Also on her stereo, according to an interview with *The Guardian*, were Thelonius Monk, Minnie Riperton, Miles Davis and Dinah Washington.

"I love Dinah," said Amy, "because she would sing all over the song, rather than just do it straight, and she could sing a standard in a gritty gospel style then do a blues and just kill everyone in the room."

The Guardian also noted some of the cultural debris littering her Camden flat, where the interview took place: a cushion decorated with a picture of Patrick Swayze, circa *Dirty Dancing*; a hairdryer; a mirror; a hole in the living room ceiling that needed the attention of a builder; and a pile of videos and DVDs that included Martin Scorsese's *Mean Streets* (maybe that's where The Ronettes obsession that would give *Back To Black* its centre started – the bar scene where Scorsese blasts 'Be My Baby'), Frank Capra's *It's A Wonderful Life* (on every depressive's top films of all time list) and, somewhat less impressively, Amy Heckerling's *Look Who's Talking Too*.

Profiling Amy in February 2004, *The Independent* again theorised that her success was a by-product of Norah Jones' colossal emergence as an artist during 2003. "Some say that if it wasn't for the flabbergasting success of Norah Jones, an artist like new Brit sensation Amy Winehouse couldn't exist. Jones has unlocked new horizons of subtle, soulful and sophisticated music, harking back to the classic heritage of jazz yet modern and broad-minded enough to embrace pop, country and hip-hop. But while she's providing a welcome refuge for listeners horrified by nu-metal and driven to apathy by prefab pop, there isn't quite enough devil in Ms Jones for anybody who wants their jazz to be risky and cutting-edge." Enter Amy Winehouse, whose jazzy sound had both those qualities. Despite the mounting critical acclaim, sales of *Frank* remained tepid while Norah Jones' album continued to sell strongly.

At the BRIT Awards ceremony on February 17, despite two nominations and high hopes by everybody in the Amy camp, she failed to win either award for which she had been nominated. In the Best British female category, Amy, Sophie Ellis Bextor, Jamelia and Annie Lennox lost out to Dido, and in the Best British urban category, Amy, Mis-Teeq, Dizzee Rascal and Big Brovas all lost out to Lemar.

On April 5, Island, by now surely hoping for that elusive breakthrough hit, released a third single from *Frank*. The latest was a double A-side featuring 'In My Bed' and 'You Sent Me Flying'. The CD single also featured 'Best Friend'. For the first time, the cover image bore some resemblance to Amy Winehouse the artist. Crouching down in a summer dress, hand to forehead, looking as though the photographer had caught her in the middle of a contemplative moment, the cover actually made a visual connection to the music. Against a city-scene backdrop, with her long, flowing hair and sullen expression she looked every bit the heartbroken young urbanite. Despite the better packaging and the double A-side assault on radio, it was another failure, reached no higher than 60 in the UK charts, three places lower than 'Take The Box'.

Nevertheless, with three singles from *Frank* now out, Amy felt more confident in her independence as an artist, and increasingly detached from the media idea that she, Katie Melua, Norah Jones and Jamie Cullum were all working in the same giddy, easy, jazz-pop frequencies. "I think that as my output increases people will realise that I'm in a class of my own," she told *The Independent* that month. "I'm different. I don't pride myself as being a great singer. I pride myself on being unique and on writing music that I would like to hear. That is what drives me."

Sure of where she was heading, she launched her first headlining solo tour (a sold-out headlining solo tour, no less) on April 21 at the Cottier Theatre in Glasgow. Reviewing the show, *The Scotsman* declared, "Unfortunately, during this gig the majority of her songs were coated in a standard issue jazz-funk veneer, which was tedious after five minutes, let alone an hour and five minutes, and her rich, mature tone was poorly served by her favoured vocal style." The review went from bad to worse, striking below the belt: "Winehouse oversang mercilessly like just another competent *Pop Idol* wannabe, mistaking vocal acrobatics for sophisticated soulful interpretation. By the time she had finished mangling each track, any melody which might have asserted itself was totally exterminated." Not content to stop there, the reviewer then took a stab at Amy's acclaimed lyric style: "As for candid lyrical revelations, the audience lapped up the one about her dead canary."

From Glasgow, the tour took in Northumbria University, Liverpool Academy, Manchester Academy 2, Nottingham Rescue Rooms, Leeds Cockpit, Norwich Waterfront, Bristol Anson Rooms, Brighton Concorde, the Warwick Arts Centre and finally, on May 3, the Shepherd's Bush Empire in London, this time headlining. At the tour's conclusion, Amy appeared alongside Jay Z, Mos Def, The Streets, Beyoncé, Dizzee Rascal and Alicia Keys at the Prince's Trust Urban Music Festival, held at the Earl Court's Arena in London over the weekend of May 8 and 9.

On May 27, the 49th annual Ivor Novello Awards ceremony was held at the Grosvenor House Hotel in central London, and Amy had been nominated for Best Contemporary Song for 'Stronger Than Me'. She was up against Dizzee Rascal for 'Jus' A Rascal' and Kylie Minogue for 'Slow'. The event celebrates the year's best in British songwriting and composing, and, unlike at the BRITs, Amy actually won the award.

In her acceptance speech, Amy said very simply: "I have to write honestly about things which happen to me and hope people can relate to that." She was delighted that her work had been recognised and, the following day, sales of *Frank* exploded. By the end of the month, sales had reached 200,000 copies in the UK and the album hit its chart peak of 13.

The award nominations continued. Amy was nominated for the 2004 Mercury Music Award for *Frank* and also for two categories at the 2004 MOBO Awards – the Best Jazz Act category (alongside Jamie Cullum, Norah Jones, Denys Baptiste and Keb' Mo') and also for UK Act of the Year (alongside Dizzee Rascal, Jamelia, Lemar, Joss Stone and The Streets). Amy was delighted because MOBO nominations meant her music was crossing over to a black audience, as she had intended. Since by choice she listened to very little music that wasn't of black origin, the MOBO nominations would have touched her the most profoundly.

At the end of June, Amy made her debut appearance at the Glastonbury festival, performing on the Jazz World stage. On the Saturday (the festival takes place over a three-day weekend, Friday to Sunday), Joss Stone and Jamie Cullum played the same stage. Amy appeared on Sunday, June 27, going on after Mikey Dread. She was followed by Bonnie Raitt and Roy Ayers, The Soft Machine legend.

Enjoying the summer festival season, Amy appeared at T In The Park, over the weekend of July 10 and 11. She performed in the King Tut's tent on the Sunday alongside Orbital and Snow Patrol, and on August 15 she appeared at the Summer Sundae Weekender in Leicester, alongside the likes of Air and Super Furry Animals. At the V Festival, over the weekend of August 18 and 19, Amy performed at the JJB/Puma arena, sharing a weekend bill with the likes of Jamelia, Kelis and Basement Jaxx.

Chasing all these festival appearances and awards excitement, Island released a fourth and final single from *Frank*, 'Fuck Me Pumps' – re-titled for single release as 'Pumps' – on August 23. As with the third single, Island opted to make it a double A-side, running 'Pumps' equal with 'Help Yourself' and backed with a live version of 'There Is No Greater Love'. The cover followed the image portrayed on the previous single, presenting Amy finally in full diva mode – sitting down, legs crossed, big hoop earrings, looking straight into the camera, hands ruffling up her hair. It was a classic movie actress pose, evoking the ghost of Marilyn Monroe or a young Sophia Loren. Ten months after *Frank* had hit shops, the marketing had fallen into place. Amy stared out from the cover, sultry, brooding and strong. The music behind the cover matched the image. Nevertheless, despite all the promising live dates and the escalating award nominations, the single still failed to put a dent in the Top 40, bottoming out no higher than number 65 on the UK singles chart.

In the first week of September, Amy performed 'Take The Box' at the Mercury Music Prize awards. She had, of course, been nominated for the prize itself, which earned the winner a cheque for £20,000, along with Franz Ferdinand, The Streets, The Zutons, Keane, Snow Patrol, Basement Jaxx, Joss Stone, Belle & Sebastian, Jamelia, Robert Wyatt and Ty. The sizeable cheque ended up going to Franz Ferdinand for their self-titled debut album.

On September 30, at the MOBO Awards ceremony at the Royal Albert Hall in central London, Amy waited with baited breath to see if her nominations would be successful. Unfortunately, it turned out to be a repeat of the BRIT awards and she lost out on both nominations. The Best Jazz Act award went to Jamie Cullum and the Best UK Act award went jointly to Jamelia and Dizzee Rascal.

To end a hectic year, during which she had done much to build her name and reputation in the UK, Amy took off on a second UK tour, opening at the Liquid Room in Newcastle on November 4. She then moved on to play at the Liverpool Academy, the Sheffield Octagon, the Newcastle Northumbria University, Nottingham Rock City, the University of East Anglia in Norwich, the Carling Academy in Birmingham, the Manchester Academy, the Folkestone Leas Cliff Hall, the Bristol Academy and the Southampton Guildhall, before closing with a final show at London's Brixton Academy on November 19.

And then Amy was at home again in her Camden flat, reeling from 13 frantic months promoting *Frank* and the album's four singles. So much had happened in so little time. Fourteen months earlier she was singing at the Cobden, in every sense an artist on the brink. And now, little over a year later, she had passed innumerable tests – singing to audiences of all sizes, shooting videos, giving interviews, touring, doing radio, having her photograph taken. *Frank* was on its way to UK sales of a quarter of a million copies. Sales had risen since the Ivor Novello award, but not so well for Island to strike a deal to release the album in the US, where the big audiences and big money and big fame awaited. Though none of her four singles had reached the Top 40, Amy Winehouse was a name on everybody's lips. She had proved her worth, worked *Frank* hard and wowed ever larger numbers of people with that voice. What now? The label was already asking her about getting started on her second album – was she ready to get down to some writing? But Amy wanted a break. She needed to get inspired before she could write another album. She needed something to happen. Preferably a calamity.

Of course, she wasn't absolutely certain that it would take a catastrophe for her to shine her brightest as a songwriter, but, soon enough, it would become clear to her, obvious in a morose, devastating way. More pressingly, she wanted head space, a chance to take stock of all that had happened in the past year. Some elements in her career were not right. She needed to figure out which ones. And when she did, the impact of those changes would ring magnificently.

Chapter Six

Love Me Or Leave Me

Early in 2005, Amy, now 21, was at her local pub, the Hawley Arms in Camden, when she crossed paths with a tattooed, rebellious young man close to two years her senior. He was a part-time gofer on music-video sets called Blake Fielder-Civil. According to a later report in *The Daily Mail*, Fielder-Civil had also worked as a part-time barman and, in terms of the work he did as a gofer, this extended to helping with make-up and hair on music-video shoots. Like Amy's, his parents had divorced. His father, Lance Fielder, was a 64-year-old retired businessman at the time Blake and Amy met. His mother, Georgette, then 40, owned a hair salon, and had long since remarried. Her second husband, Giles Civil, was a 40-year-old headmaster, and the couple lived in Newark in Nottinghamshire with their two teenage sons.

"I spend a lot of time playing pool and listening to jukebox music," Amy told *Rolling Stone* in 2007, when she was asked about the circumstances of their first encounter at the pub.

Amy and Blake embarked on a brief, intense relationship. "I used to smoke a lot of weed," she said. "I suppose if you have an addictive personality then you go from one poison to the other. He doesn't smoke weed, so I started drinking more and not smoking as much. And because of that I just enjoyed stuff more."

The couple would meet at the pub, drink, smoke cigarettes, play pool, keep the jukebox busy with their favourite music. Her preferred listening at the time included old Motown hits, blues standards and Sixties pop nuggets by all-girl groups such as The Ronettes, The Shirelles and The Crystals.

"When I fell in love with Blake, there was Sixties music around us a lot," she said, adding that she became obsessed with the pulpy relationship dramas cast as two-minute snappy female pop gems such as The Angels' 'My Boyfriend's Back', The Ronettes' 'Be My Baby', The Shangri-Las' 'Leader Of The Pack' and The Crystals' 'Then He Kissed Me'. Those songs would be filed away in her inspiration filter and reappear as a major influence on the songs, sound and look of her second album. Meanwhile, her relationship with Blake was turbulent from the offset, as she told *The Sun* in 2006: "I shouldn't have been in a relationship with him because he was already involved with someone else a bit too close to home."

Despite the precariousness of association, the couple were madly in love and spent their every waking moment together. Amy later told *The Observer* that he was her ideal type. "If I'm checking out a man I'll usually go for someone who is at least five nine, with dark hair, dark eyes and loads of tattoos (that was Blake)."

The relationship raged for close to six months. Then, external pressures brought their love tumbling down and Blake and Amy split up. Amy was devastated. Blake went back to his old girlfriend. Amy drank heavily.

"I was really depressed," she told *The Daily Record* in 2006. "I was in love with someone and it fell through. A lot of it was to do with bad choices and misgivings. We were both to blame for the split."

Miserable at home, she began writing about her heartbreak. The songs quickly began to accumulate, taking the shape of what would become *Back To Black*.

"Back to black is when you've finished a relationship," she told *The Sun* in 2006. "And you go back to what's comfortable for you. My ex went back to his girlfriend and I went back to drinking and dark times."

While heartbroken, Amy also had to deal with pressure from her management and label to work on a new album. They wanted her to get writing, get into a studio. There was also concern at her drinking in the wake of her break-up with Blake. Her management suggested she cool the drinking down. Amy failed to heed this advice and carried on drowning her sorrows while privately, writing candid break-up songs. Then she began to lose weight. Having not seen her for a while, her manager Nick Godwin was shocked at how much weight she had lost.

"I was definitely drinking too much," she told *The Daily Record* at the time of *Back To Black*'s release. "I've always had a high tolerance for alcohol. The kind of states I was getting myself into was a joke. I'll admit it was a joke. My friends would find me at six o'clock on a Saturday night drunk already. I shouldn't have been drunk at that time. I'd be wrecked from the day before, having stayed up all night and I'd still be up. Or I'd have passed out at five o'clock. It wasn't very healthy."

Eventually, her management stepped in and leaned on Amy to seek help or at least advice. The upshot of their intervention was that Amy agreed to meet with an addiction counsellor at a rehab centre.

"I was having a particularly nasty time with things and just drinking and drinking," she told *The Sun*. "My management decided to stop buying for me and said they were taking me to rehab. I asked my dad if he thought I needed to go. He said no but I should give it a try. So I did, for just 15 minutes. I went in, said hello and explained that I drink because I am in love and have fucked up the relationship. Then I walked out."

This episode, of course, was the basis for 'Rehab', which was written off the cuff in New York, in early 2006, and became the hit that announced the arrival of *Back To Black*. Talking with *The Sunday Tribune* in 2007, she gave a slightly different account of how she ended up seeing the counsellor. She said that the meeting came about after a bust-up with Tyler James, her old friend from Sylvia Young's.

"We were so close that he did so much for me for nothing and I love him and I respect that," she said. "He's still like my big brother. I think he was at the end of his rope. After the end of a particularly nasty drunken episode he called my dad who said, 'You gotta come and see me and stay a couple of days'. So I said, 'OK I'll come and stay.'"

Her father and Tyler James both suggested that she make an appointment at a rehab facility for an assessment, to try and ascertain if she had any issues of dependency and, if so, whether they needed to be treated.

"I walked in and the guy said, 'Why do you think you are here?' I said, 'I am drinking a lot, I'm in love and I fucked it up and I'm a manic depressive'. Then he asked me if I thought I was an alcoholic and I said, 'Maybe'. I didn't want to say no because he might think I'm in denial. He started talking and I kind of switched off and 15 minutes later I went, 'Thanks very much'. I genuinely believe that if you can't sort yourself out no one else can. Afterwards, I asked my dad, 'Do you think I need to go to rehab, really?' And he said, 'No.'"

So Amy went back to Camden, went back to being heartbroken, went back to trying to beat the clinical depression, went back to drinking, went back to writing, went back to being alone. "All the songs [on *Back To Black*] are about the state of my relationship at the time with Blake," she told *Rolling Stone* in 2006. "I had never felt the way I feel about him about anyone in my life. It was very cathartic, because I felt terrible about the way we treated each other. I thought we'd never see each other again. I wanted to die."

Amy quite seriously had the feeling that she'd lost the love of her life, that special one who made her life complete. The drama of the broken relationship and the rehab experience arrived at her finger-tips, made for great music as she tried to sing and strum her way out of this personal crisis.

To get out of her dark head space, she accepted an invitation to perform at the Cornbury Music Festival, which was held between July 9 and 10 at Cornbury Farm Estate in Charlbury, Oxfordshire. Amy appeared on the main stage on the Saturday alongside Bonnie Tyler and Joe Cocker. Then she went back to writing songs in her Camden flat, appealing to music to make her better.

"The songs I wrote on the album are from times when I was so messed up in the head, I had literally hit... not rock bottom, I hate to use such a phrase, since I'm sure I will sink lower at some point. But

I was clinically depressed and I managed to get something I'm so proud of out of something that was so horrible" she told *Entertainment Weekly* in 2007.

As anyone who has experienced clinical depression knows, the illness settles gloomily over an individual, effortlessly robs months of time without the sufferer ever really knowing that time is slipping away. It puts everything on a blue pause.

Amy emerged later that year to play a set in the name of charity at her old haunt, the Cobden, on Saturday November 19, a show arranged by Young Jewish Care's The Set Committee. A review appeared in *The Jewish Chronicle* five days later explaining that Amy had flown in especially from Miami to perform for free at the fundraiser. Amy performed three songs, and all proceeds from the event, which raised close to £7,500, went to the Holocaust Survivors' Centre. The review noted that the show was opened by a Robbie Williams tribute band and that by the time Amy took to the stage in "skinny jeans" and a T-shirt, her "unsmiling side was on show". She sang solo, sitting on a stool, strumming and plucking at an acoustic guitar, opening with 'Take The Box' and closing with 'You Sent Me Flying'. The review quoted Neil Miller, co-chair of the Set Committee, on his thoughts of her performance: "Amy was fantastic. It was a phenomenal evening."

Meanwhile, her management contract with Brilliant 19 Ltd was about to expire and she decided against renewing the deal. She needed new direction, new management, a fresh future and, artistically, to move away from *Frank*, from the overt jazzy sound, and to pursue a new style. She also wanted to get away from the association with Simon Fuller, which she was sick of having to explain. Parallel to a likely management change, as 2005 crept to a close she found herself in possession of four or five very strong new songs, including 'Love Is A Losing Game'.

It had become obvious to her now that she needed to be in pain to write. "I have to feel very strongly about something before I can write about it," she told *The Sunday Herald* in 2007. "But when I start, I'm on a roll. The album [*Back To Black*] took me about six months to write."

At the start of 2006, she officially parted company with Brilliant 19 Ltd and signed a new deal with Raye Cosbert at Metropolis Music. In 2007, *Music Week* quoted Guy Moot, the Managing Director of EMI Music Publishing, as saying with the gift of hindsight: "There are two pivotal moments in Amy's career: the introduction of Raye Cosbert and of Mark Ronson."

Cosbert arrived as her manager from a position of industry savvy and experience, and the Metropolis Music offices, based in north London, were handy for Amy, close to her flat in Camden. He had already been working with Amy for several years, promoting her live shows since she first headed out in support of *Frank* in 2003. They'd got along well, forming a good professional relationship, so when Amy was suddenly without management, the decision to sign with Cosbert, while not the obvious first choice, suddenly seemed like a logical idea. Cosbert told *Music Week* that he and Amy had a chance meeting in Camden during this unsettling era. Amy told him what had happened with Brilliant 19 Ltd and, in turn, Cosbert told her that he was "doing the odd thing management wise". From there, the pair came to a natural realisation – Amy was without a manager and Cosbert had been dipping his toe in that field, so why not partner up? Each respected the other and knew the other was a solid and interesting bet.

Cosbert joined Metropolis in 1989 and, at the time he became Amy's manager, had many glowing credits on his CV, having promoted acts and artists of the calibre of Blur, Robbie Williams, Massive Attack and Björk. He first made a name for himself in the Eighties by putting Public Enemy on at the Docklands Arena, the first rap show to sell out an arena-sized venue in the UK. Since then, he had worked closely with artists such as Lynden David Hall, Goldie Lookin' Chain and Bronze Age Fox, while continuing to break new boundaries, including becoming the first promoter to work with London's Royal Opera House. By becoming both her manager and her live promoter, Cosbert would be her main point of contact with the industry, and could apply his strategic vision over her entire career.

Once Cosbert was officially managing Amy, EMI was delighted. Guy Moot told *Music Week* of the new management: "Raye coming in put a real period of stability into the whole campaign. He is incredibly calm and by remaining calm, he focuses on what the goals are and at the same time harnesses the more erratic artistic moments that Amy has."

A year later, Amy would tell CMU Beats Bar why she left Brilliant 19 Ltd and transferred her interests to Cosbert. "I was definitely unhappy with my management," she said. "I was on a learning curve and through that I discovered I was with the wrong managers. Your management tend to be the go-between between you and your label, so because I was having problems with my managers I was going to have problems with the label. But most of those problems weren't really there. I didn't want to talk to my managers, which meant I never spoke to the label, which probably meant they thought I was being awkward, that I didn't care. But now I've got the management thing fixed I get on brilliantly with my label."

Under Cosbert's wing, Amy was ready to move ahead with a new album. She had taken the best part of a year out of her career, a chance to catch her breath after the *Frank* campaign. She had played one or two shows but had mostly been caught up in her relationship dramas with Blake. Now, with a cluster of strong songs, all chronicling the break-up with Blake and the personal crisis the split had caused, Cosbert was in a position to talk with Darcus Beese and get the new record under way.

"I did take a year off before I really started work on the new album," Amy later told CMU Beats Bar. "The label kept saying, 'So, do you want to make another album?' But I just wasn't ready. I had about three or four songs together but that wasn't enough to get started properly. I only really got to that stage when I met Mark [Ronson]."

At first, it seemed logical that she go into the studio again with Salaam Remi. There was talk of him producing the entire new album. But then Beese arranged for Amy to meet a hot DJ and emerging producer, Mark Ronson, at the beginning of 2006. Like Amy, Ronson was signed to EMI publishing.

"They suggested we should work together," Amy told CMU Beats Bar in 2006, "possibly because they were desperate to get something new out of me. I wasn't too convinced at first. I kind of thought of Mark as some white guy who tried too hard. But we met, and he was much more friendly than I expected, and we had a lot more in common music wise that I had thought."

Ronson was born in London in September 1975 and raised in St John's Wood. His mother, the socialite/writer Ann Dexter-Jones, and father, Laurence Ronson, split up when he was a child. His mother married again, to Mick Jones, guitarist of AOR group Foreigner, who scored the major 1981 hit, 'Waiting For A Girl Like You'. When Ronson was eight, he moved with his mother to New York, where he became close friends with Sean Lennon. Jewish, Ronson had his bar mitzvah in New York in 1989. After playing guitar in a rock-funk outfit whose one claim to fame was opening for The Spin Doctors, he switched to turntables and started working as a DJ on the club scene in New York in 1993. He loved hip-hop and developed a reputation as a DJ who mixed eclectic sounds. By the time he was introduced to Amy Winehouse, he'd hit the celebrity circuit, Djing at P Diddy's 29th birthday party and at the 2006 wedding of Tom Cruise and Katie Holmes. Moving into production, he aspired to make sounds in the same way as his favourite producers, Quincy Jones, Rick Rubin and RZA of Wu-Tang Clan. He told *The Jewish Chronicle* in 2007 of the affinity he felt between himself, a white Jewish man, and the black artists he reveres: "There's a love affair between Jews and black music, especially in America. It comes down to some kind of outsider culture."

His breakthrough as a producer came with working on Nikka Costa's 2001 album *Like A Feather*, which featured the hit 'Everybody's Got Their Something'. That netted Ronson a contract with Elektra Records, for whom he released his debut album, *Here Comes The Fuzz*, a multi-collaborative project that spawned the hit single 'Ooh Wee', featuring Nate Dogg, Ghostface Killah and Trife Da God. In the run-up to *Back To Black*, he had most recently produced Lily Allen's *Alright, Still*; Christina Aguilera's *Back To Basics* and Robbie Williams' *Rudebox*.

Amy was nervous about what Ronson would be like. "She thought I was going to be some older Jewish guy or something," Ronson told *Spin* in July 2007. "I don't know if she thought I'd be like Rick

Rubin or maybe Leonard Cohen. We listened to everything, like Earl & The Cadillacs and The Angels, and just started talking the way music geeks do when they get together."

After that first meeting, Ronson began working on what would become 'Back To Black', the title track. His head buzzing with The Shirelles, The Shangri-Las and The Angels, he got to work in his studio. "That night, I did the drumbeat and piano part and put tons of reverb on the tambourine. [Amy's] deceivingly nonchalant and when I played it for her the next day, she said, 'It's wicked', but I couldn't tell if she meant it. Then she was like, 'This is what I want my album to sound like.'"

From there on, the work was very organic. "I'd play something I'd been working on," Amy told CMU Beats Bar, "or a song I like and then overnight he'd think about it and come back to me with an idea or suggestion or another song he liked. Once me and Mark started doing that stuff I was ready to start work on a new album, and that's what we spent the first half of the year doing."

Settling into a groove, Amy dropped into Ronson's studio on a daily basis to work on material. Amy would strum songs on an acoustic guitar and Ronson would try out different arrangements. Eventually, they knew the direction they wanted to take. "The reason everyone goes back to those Motown records," Ronson told *Spin*, "is that there were amazing musicians playing together in a room, and that's what we tried to do."

Working fast, they laid down basic tracks in a mere three weeks. Parallel to working with Ronson in New York, Amy would also fly down to Miami to work on the other half of the album with Salaam Remi. The label had liked the twin approach of Commissioner Gordon and Remi during the making of *Frank* and were keen to repeat the formula for *Back To Black*. As before, Remi invited Amy to his house in Miami, where they worked on tracks at his studio. He had so much equipment at the studio by this time that he called it the "instrument zoo". There, they set about finding the vintage sound she was after. All of the basic tracks for his half of the album were recorded in his living room, with cables and wires trailing upstairs to a bedroom.

"The songs were twisted around that format in the same tempo and were lyrically all the same," he told *Remix* magazine. "What pulls the album together is Amy's confidence and what she wanted to hear."

Once her vocal tracks were down, Remi set about mastering the vintage sound. His engineer, Frank 'Esoes' Socorro, treated the snare-drum until it had the sound of records released in the early Sixties. Remi then studied the techniques of legendary Atlantic engineer Tom Dowd and got in touch with Jim Gaines, a former sound engineer at Stax, to pick his brain about methods and strategies he used on those classic Stax recordings. Remi particularly wanted to ask Gaines how he'd recommend getting a crackly old vinyl LP sound.

"It came down to putting a Neumann U 87 microphone on a snare right in between the hi-hats," Remi told *Remix* magazine. "Pretty much letting hi-hats and snare go into one better mic rather than two mics where you're trying to separate the sound. He recorded the songs in one room and moved the mics around."

The mood, in terms of musical inspiration, reflected the era when Amy was dating Blake and listening to music on the jukebox in the Hawley Arms.

"I wrote my first album when I was listening to a lot of jazz, a lot of hip-hop," she told *Entertainment Weekly* in 2007. "When I listen to my second album, I was listening to a substantially smaller amount of music – soul, doo-wop, girl groups – and it shows. I was just listening to very different types of music when I did two different albums."

While working with Ronson, she suddenly wrote 'Rehab' off the cuff. The pair of them were walking down a street in New York's Soho district when the phrase came to Amy. "I sang the hook," she told *Papermag* in 2007. "I sang it as a joke. Mark started laughing, saying, 'That's so funny. That's so funny, Amy. Whose song is that, man?' I told him, 'I just wrote it off the top of my head. I was just joking'. And he said, 'It would be so cool if you had a whole song about rehab'. I said, 'Well, I could write it right now. Let's go to the studio'. And that was it."

Ronson loved the track, as he told *NY Mag* in 2007. "There's a way that white singers with really good, soulful voices, definitely interpret soul in their own way. Winehouse, with 'Rehab', starts with a real belting kind of Ray Charles–ish blues, but then when it goes into the verse, she goes into this sort of Beatles minor-y chords, you know? I like both of those things. Stevie Wonder doing 'We Can Work It Out' by The Beatles is one of my favorite records of all time."

Once their cluster of songs had an identity – somewhere between The Ronettes as produced by Phil Spector and the records of Seventies soul legend Donny Hathaway – Ronson racked his brains for the right way to arrange and record the songs. Then it came to him and he brought in The Dap-Kings, the nine-piece house band at Daptones studio in Brooklyn, and had them cut their input live, working with Amy's guitar and vocal tracks. The Dap-Kings, known for their funk/soul revivalist spirit and music, record using old fashioned equipment instead of the plethora of digital technology and software available today. Hence, the lovely vintage sound of the records they record with singer Sharon Jones. When Mark Ronson brought them in to work on *Back To Black*, Sharon Jones was not involved and the band were billed simply as The Dap-Kings. The band grew out of The Soul Providers, formed in the middle Nineties by Phillip Lehman and Gabriel Roth (aka Bosco "Bass" Mann). While recording, Lehman and Roth hired a backing singer from Augusta, Georgia called Sharon Jones. Lehman and Roth then launched a label, Desco Records, based in Brooklyn. They were also running a studio. On Desco, they set about releasing 45rpm vinyl singles by various artists who shared their retro soul/funk aesthetic.

In 2000, Lehman and Roth parted ways over internal business conflicts and each founded their own new label. Roth, at this time head engineer at Desco, co-founded Daptone Records with Neal Sugarman, a saxophonist. By then The Soul Providers had split and out of their ashes a new band formed called The Dap-Kings. They released their debut album, *Dip Dappin With Sharon Jones & The Dap-Kings*, in 2001, and quickly earned a reputation as the hottest live old-school soul/funk retro act in the US. In 2003, label and studio moved to a rundown two-bedroom house in Bushwick, Brooklyn, where they installed their studio, The Daptone Recording Studio, complete with its days-gone-by recording equipment and a 16-track analogue tape machine. Then, in 2005, the same year the Dap-Kings released their second album, *Naturally*, savvy DJ Mark Ronson, knowing that collaborators of his like Ghostface Killah worshipped and on occasion sampled The Dap-Kings, fell too for the beautiful old sounds emerging from Daptone Studios.

Ronson then befriended Gabriel Roth – two Jewish men bonding over a shared love of black music. Over the coming months, Ronson would work repeatedly with the Daptone staff and The Dap-Kings. He would take three projects to them: the Lily Allen album, his second solo album *Version* (a collection of cover versions with star guest vocalists) and Amy Winehouse's *Back To Black*. He knew that their soul/funk spirit would perfectly complement Amy's songs of romantic hopes dashed, and in Gabriel Roth, a very talented sound engineer, he saw a logical collaborator, especially in helping Amy achieve her vintage Sixties/early Seventies sound. Roth would end up overseeing band arrangements in partnership with Ronson on four tracks on the album: 'Rehab', 'Back To Black', 'Love Is A Losing Game' and 'Wake Up Alone' – three of which would go on to become hit singles. In all four cases, the songs ooze the Daptone vintage sound. When the album came out, to everyone's embarrassment, songs recorded at Daptone Studios were listed in the CD sleeve notes as having been recorded at "Dapking Studios". Any dented egos were surely smoothed over when Amy invited The Dap-Kings to go on the road as her backing band for her first US tour in early 2007.

Aside from The Dap-Kings/Daptone Studios family, other musicians made contributions, like Victor Axelrod, who is credited with having added "handclaps and Wurlitzer" to 'Rehab' and 'You Know I'm No Good' and piano on 'Rehab', 'You Know I'm No Good', 'Back To Black', 'Love Is A Losing Game', 'Some Unholy War' and 'Addicted'. Axelrod, also known as Ticklah, was born and raised in Brooklyn. He studied jazz in his late teens with Mike Longo while expanding his interest in ska, reggae and dub. Particular inspirations included Augustus Pablo, Dennis Bovell and King Tubby. He played with various New York-based ska and reggae outfits before doing time with acid jazz band Cooly's Hot Box and Michael G's Special Request. More recently, he had played with The Soul Providers and

The Dap-Kings while writing, performing and recording solo out-ings under the name Ticklah. Axelrod has also long been a seminal member of The Easy Star All-Stars with Michael G – a collective of top-rank reggae musicians based around the New York area. He got a call from Ronson to come and join The Dap-Kings in the studio while working on *Back To Black*.

"As a DJ, he had been checking out the records that were being made at Daptone Studios in Brooklyn," says Axelrod. "And I guess really appreciated the sonic approach and also just the style of play and musicianship of the people in the stable. He thought that a pair-ing of this group of musicians with Gabe's engineering approach would work with this batch of songs."

Ronson then played Axelrod and the other musicians demos, where demos existed, to give them a feel for the material.

"We starting working them out. That's not to say he never said anything, but part of the reason he was coming to us was that he would be able to let us get on with it, I guess. He had chord charts, he had the demos, so it wasn't like we were gonna have no idea how to play them the way he wanted to hear them."

What kind of instruction did Ronson give the band?

"He would listen to some of the things I was doing and just say, OK, keep that note on top. I don't recall him having to really talk to us about anything."

Sometimes, session work can be a punch-in job. This was not the case for Axelrod when working on *Back To Black*.

"I remember being really pleasantly surprised at how much I liked the songs [while] listening to the demos with Amy's voice."

The band worked most of the time with chord charts so Ronson could record them playing live as bass, drums, piano and two guitars.

"The arrangement of the tunes was already pretty set. And I don't recall hearing demos for every tune. I remember we had chord charts for every song, but I think Gabe had demos of Amy singing and play-ing guitar and made chord charts from that."

Axelrod remembers certain songs in particular. "I remember the demo of 'Back To Black', that was already very much in the style. We listened to the demo and sort of set a vibe from that. It had a Phil

Spector feel. On 'You Know I'm No Good', we looked at the chord chart and maybe talked some more and then started playing."

Most of The Dap-Kings' work was over in a day. Axelrod, having more of a musician-at-large role, worked with Ronson for several days.

"I came in a second day and did Wurtlitzer on 'Rehab', because I played piano on all the songs. I also did handclaps. Mark had an engineer on handclaps too, later that day. I think it was two days. And then Mark took the tapes to England to add some of the orchestra stuff."

At the end of the first day, Axelrod, not knowing who Ronson was, went home and Googled the DJ/producer. "I was kinda shocked. All Gabe had said was that there's a DJ/producer guy who's hot shit coming in here for a session."

When working on 'Rehab', Axelrod had no idea he was helping shape a track that would become a global catchphrase. "I didn't know a tune like 'Rehab' or something like that would catch. Something like 'You Know I'm No Good', I'm actually not surprised that a song like that would catch on here [in the US]. But you know, certain things will fly in England that won't fly here."

Axelrod does not recall Ronson talking much about Phil Spector or the all-girl groups who had inspired Amy so much. "I never in my life listened to that music. I've heard all that just because at some point you're gonna hear it on radio or in the movies, but it's not like I own any of those records. But thankfully I was able to play some stuff that Mark really liked in that style. But the thing is, myself and the other guys who played on the records could all appreciate the music, even if it's so far back that we don't actually listen to it. That era of music is not really anything that I like to listen to. But it's all close enough in terms of the connections, like blues underpinnings. From that, we could all apply our sound. A tune like 'You Know I'm No Good', that was a lot easier. A tune like 'Rehab' was a little bit tougher, because we've never really played like that."

The first song they worked on was doomed love anthem 'Back To Black'. "We had actually had two takes of that, because the tempo of that tune and the way it flies along makes it a challenging tune to play, not because it's so complicated, but to maintain that sort of feel, that particular kind of momentum. That did take some work, and it was a bit delicate to keep the balance between ourselves as we played. I think we did a bunch of takes of that before Mark felt we got it. I don't think that happened with any of the others."

The most natural song for the vintage soul outfit to walk through was 'Love Is A Losing Game'. "I recall that one coming out easy, I think we all enjoyed playing those chord changes. I don't recall hearing Amy's vocal, I think we did that one from the chord chart and just settled into the mood. That's actually my favourite track on the record."

A few weeks after Axelrod finished his contributions to the record, Ronson called him back to the studio to work on 'He Can Only Hold Her'. "I don't think that was going to be on the album, but then at the last minute they wanted to stick it on and if I'm not mistaken we listened to a demo by Salaam Remi. I just remember that we listened to a demo of that song with a completely different production style, just to hear what the chords were. And that one was a snap. We just snuck that one right out."

Like Amy, Axelrod found Ronson a very intuitive producer. "One of the nice things about working with Mark is that he actually knows chords, he knows harmony and he's got good ears for, say, inversions, extensions. I've worked with producers and they don't know anything about music, and they can't communicate things about it other than 'I like it' or 'I don't'. Mark's pretty laid-back and kinda let things unfold; he was quick to hear when things are right and then press those things out a bit more. Somebody like Mark might reference a record that the guys know. He definitely speaks our language. It was easy all round. Whether it was actually speaking in specific terms about don't play this ninth on that chord."

Down in Miami, Troy Genius once again got a call from Salaam Remi, inviting him to come and drum on his half of the new record. Genius got in his car, cruised up the highway and was at Remi's studio inside of 20 minutes. Remi again entrusted him to take the tracks where they needed to go.

"*Back To Black* was basically the same [as making *Frank*] because Amy had the same jazzy feel," recalls Genius. "So it wasn't really all that different on the second album. We just sat in the studio and we listened to it and we talked about what kind of feel, what kind of ideas. And then on other songs, I'd just go in there and do about four or five different types of stuff and we'd take whichever one [worked best]. Because we were working with Pro Tools so we could always add different tracks."

Genius sees his role in the making of the album as being quite clearly defined.

"I think I played a major part in constructing a groove, or particular flavour to what she was singing about."

The little guidance that Remi did need to give Genius was typically abstract.

"Salaam was always mentioning a grainy feel with a little red and a little orange. All those textures have a definite meeting. An orangey red is more of a warm feeling, you know. Grainy means that it has a little edge to it. He knows how to get that in the final product."

Nowhere did that warm feeling shine brighter than on 'Just Friends', with its reggae groove tailor-made for Troy Genius. "That was really a blessing to be playing reggae on the album like that. And to give it such an orthodox feel, a Seventies feel, it was honour to reproduce that."

Throughout the sessions, Genius worked solely with Remi. "I haven't met any of the other musicians. I just come in and do my part. Just like how we do any other project. He calls me up. I go down there. I do it with him."

It was while Amy's second album was being mixed that she realised she'd created something very special. Darcus Beese at Island was excited because the record had a slew of potential hit singles, each as strong as the next. The twin attack of Remi and Ronson had created dynamic material, produced with imagination and sonic flair. And lyrically it was a concept album of sorts, all the songs looping on the emotional fall-out of the same broken love affair.

Chapter Seven

Back To Black

Compared with *Frank*, *Back To Black* came hurtling out of the start-ing gate, very sure of who and what it was about. This was Amy Winehouse reinvented as deep-voiced entertainer, a stax of a beehive rising from her head like an erupting volcano. The mere title of the first single from the album tapped the moment. At the time, gossip maga-zines and tabloid newspapers were filled to bursting with accounts of celebrities riding at all levels of infamy on their way to rehab, in rehab, getting out of rehab, dealing with life out of rehab, on their way back to rehab or getting out of rehab yet again. The song took the pulse of this trend, dropping Amy into the thick of the moment.

In other words, she and Ronson had crafted a song that defined an aspect of an era, a song that perfectly captured the mood. It was a dys-functional pop anthem for our dysfunctional times, and it provided the soundtrack to the yo-yoing rehab escapades of headline-grabbing celebrities such as Lindsay Lohan, Britney Spears, Robbie Williams and, especially, Kate Moss and Pete Doherty. It was a song whose pro-tagonist prides herself on getting turned away from a rehab centre, and – it has to be said – a song that has taken on an ominous new meaning in light of Amy Winehouse's own escapades during 2007.

Beneath her incredibly "of today" story, listen to those layers upon layers of Sixties soul and Phil Spector-produced, post doo-wop, all-girl pop heaven. The whole song shakes with its wealth of references. Otis Redding. The Ronettes. Shirley Bassey. Lauryn Hill. Macy Gray. Aretha Franklin. Marvin Gaye. The Temptations. Missy Elliott. Mary J. Blige. The Angels. James Brown. Nina Simone. Erykah Badu. The Supremes. Tina Turner. The Shirelles. Sam Cooke. Martha & The Vandellas. It sounds like every classic soul and rock and pop song of the Sixties in one tidy package yet it has a modern sensibility. Of its time and timeless. Of today and steeped in yesterday.

The whole song careens along with its carefully distorted edges, pitching itself somewhere between The Vandellas' 'Nowhere To Run', Sam Cooke's 'Twistin' The Night Away', The Angels' 'My Boyfriend's Back', Tina Turner's 'Nutbush City Limits', The Ronettes' 'Recipe For Love', The Eagles' 'Life In The Fast Lane' and many other classic songs. The unique feat of 'Rehab' is that it was a classic before it even reached record shops. Ronson had stacked it with vintage elements, made it *sound* like a classic, built it on unfamiliar/familiar sounds that teased the listener into an encyclopaedia of musical references that were cleverly implied yet not actually a part of the song itself: an original composition in every sense. Yet the hummability factor nags and sets up a grid of possible comparisons and references.

What the song did above all else was catapult Amy out of the jazz/soul ghetto of *Frank* and into the mainstream. The title was a gamble – would it cross over to mass-market pop audiences with the taboo-encircled title, or would the morals of millions snap tight and not want to hear tales of a 23-year-old woman being told to seek help from a treatment centre over issues connected with addictive drugs and alcohol? Yet the track spoke boldly and candidly to the entire global pop market. Here was a singer who, instead of letting tabloid reporters eagerly unmask her private life, decided to cut to the chase and use any possible speculation about her lifestyle as inspiration for a song.

'Rehab' tells a simple story based on real events in Amy's life: the occasion when her former management company expressed their concern that she was drinking too much and suggested she at least go and meet with an addiction counsellor at a rehab centre. So she went and the counsellor heard her out, asked questions and ended up concluding that she was not an alcoholic, but instead, as the song reveals, suffering through a depressive phase relating to breaking up with her boyfriend.

The song made a pitch for a larger audience. Sales of *Frank* had been significant, but the album hadn't even been released in the US. The label knew it needed to lift Amy out of the marginal groove she had been pursuing and adapt to the time. The new-jazz boom had already passed and critics and record buyers were no longer holding Jamie Cullum, Amy Winehouse and Norah Jones up as a trio representing a fresh and young new run at the legendary pastures of jazz.

And 'Rehab' was the song that was going to check all the boxes of a new Amy: retro, yes, so not likely to isolate her fans who liked the old/new sound-clash of *Frank*. Hip, because Mark Ronson was at the controls, which would give Amy an instant dose of credibility. Catchy in a way that *Frank* wasn't. Pop in a way that *Frank* wasn't. Classic in a way that baby boomers would take to. Imaginatively produced in a way that *Frank* wasn't. Listen to how Ronson works that Brian Wilson/Phil Spector wall of sound, giving 'Rehab' this skyscrapery texture, making Amy's voice sound like it is looming over the whole world. Voice as Godzilla moment. Candid in the way that *Frank* was, but more universal.

Rather than the songs reading as the diary entries of a 19-year-old north London girl into Nas, Lauryn Hill, The Beastie Boys and Ella Fitzgerald, living and having fun in Camden, *Back To Black* sounds mature by comparison, the moping break-up songs implicit with emotional depth, unexpected humour, the depression-stricken, dolorous mood of a best-selling memoir like Lauren Slater's *Prozac Diary*. And the album also taps into the confessional era, the age of taboo-busting openness about just about everything imaginable, especially sex, substance abuse and mental illness. 'Rehab' in particular is a furiously melodic song emblematic of a specific moment in time in a specific part of the western world.

Breathless, fun, fresh, kicking off with that distorted Sixties pump organ, the other obvious big change since *Frank* is the range of Amy's voice. She sings it low now, deep, dark, potent, as if from the belly, whereas on *Frank*, she sang higher. On 'Rehab', she checks Ray Charles and soul legend Donny Hathaway – in some ways, vocalist frameworks that she spends the album singing within.

The song asks listeners: where's your line? Where's your edge? Where's your boundary? What in your opinion constitutes enough, too much? She made the song a tease: what if that trip to a rehab centre was on shaky sand? How did she present herself? In what state of mind would she have been in to even go in the first place? Who entertains such a suggestion?

The British media ate up the dare. So, Amy Winehouse tantalised them, why do you think I really took up that meeting at the treatment centre? Why do you think I went? Am I telling you how it went as it really happened? Is my music really this naked? Do I really sing my life straight on this album?

Track two, 'You Know I'm No Good', literally stomps with delicious wedges of brass. The song plays it cool, rides a beat that Rolling Stone Mick Jagger (an Amy fan) would covet in a flash, shuffles itself into being with a wallop of a drumbeat, the drummer keeping an unusual beat. The bass sounds distorted, the way it tends to sound distorted on vintage reggae recordings (think of those Studio One releases), the frequency of the instrument and tone and volume of the amplifier overloading the song. Under that, a lovely swirl of psychedelic guitar played through a flanger – a classic trippy Sixties touch. Again, as with 'Rehab', Ronson brilliantly crafts a song that does not sound like it was recorded in 2006. It sounds like it was cut somewhere between 1967-1972 and that no one involved with the track could possibly be anything other than American and, for that matter, black. Of course, this is where The Dap-Kings come in, with their vintage soul flavour, throwing wonderful soul grooves all over Ronson's half of the album. Even so, Ronson and Amy are the ones leading this track.

The lyric – a pile-up of references to the great British institutions of the pint of beer, a take-away portion of chips and James Bond actor Roger Moore – again sees Amy calling out the events of her life specific to a backdrop of London, 2006. The effect created two layers.

The music, 100% American. The lyrics, for the most part British. The label must have heard early demos for this very British/very American record and seen dollar signs and pound signs flashing feverishly in tandem. An ambition – to break American audiences with *Back To Black* – was fired up. The songs, executives must have thought, should in principle cross over. Even if it would mean breaking her to American radio, press, audiences as effectively a new artist, despite her mounting celebrity at home in the UK.

The third track, 'Me & Mr Jones', starts brilliantly, with the British slang term "fuckery" slipping into the lyrics. Against the classic doo-wop/Phil Spector/Ronettes wall of explicitly American sound, Amy's Britishness screams out. It sounds like Hugh Grant bumbling in a feel-good US-set film against a soundtrack of vintage American music. Most particularly, it references Phil Spector's 1963 collection of Christmas songs, *A Christmas Gift For You From Phil Spector*, which features songs by The Ronettes, Darlene Love, The Crystals and Bob. B. Soxx & The Blue Jeans. It begins with a doo-wop chorus of backing singers and a strummed guitar and ends with the hiss of tambourines. Amy checks the failings of the boyfriend to whom she's wailing her expressions of heartache: top of the list being him standing her up and causing her to miss a show by rapper Slick Rick. As a song, it's a showcase for her voice, as she hollers and yelps, croons and growls over the sticky, stomping rhythm of the band, the backing singers covering her with a wall of vintage purrs and silky smooth embellishment.

'Just Friends' is typical of a collaboration with Salaam Remi. Of all the tracks on *Back To Black*, it sounds closest to the sound of *Frank*, Amy singing over a sunny reggae beat held down by Troy Genius. At times, the song reveals a ska dimension, referencing Amy's fondness for The Specials.

The title track, 'Back To Black', opens like a Supremes classic, beautiful dancing piano, tambourine, jaunty bass and, floating at the centre, Amy's soulful, haunted vocal. It's one of the most explicit love songs about the break-up with Blake. The chorus, bells ringing out the doom, is exquisitely stacked by Mark Ronson, a Spector-ish pile-up of chimes and apocalyptic pop shadings. Vocally, Amy is rubbing shoulders with Shirley Bassey here, singing her lungs out, torch-song style, in a manner fit for a James Bond film theme. The middle eight, all spaghetti western melodrama and tambourine taps, is brilliant and sly, a humorous send-up of the seriousness of the lyric. The title, of course, speaks of the narrator's return to depression and loneliness, dark emotional terrain, after her man leaves her and returns to his former lover.

Track six, 'Love Is A Losing Game', is the sweetest song on the album, a smooth homage to vintage soul soundscapes. The Dap-Kings are in their element here, and their playing is effortless, the perfect shade of blue. Amy's vocal, understated, is simple, the pure channelling of sadness. Lyrically, she sings her heart out, honest, candid, playing with the words. The way she expresses each phrase is truly gifted, teasing out syllables, playing all for maximum emotional impact. It's also a song where, stylistically, all her Donny Hathaway references come to fruition. The strings, the clipped guitar, the snare drum banging in the verses, the racked vocal, the soft bass, the raindrop piano playing – all of it creates a perfect bummed-out mood, a sublime Seventies soul record.

Amy's vocal on 'Tears Dry On Their Own' is deep, growling, the jazziest on the record. The verses are dark, tumbling from line to line, with Amy at times achieving the improbable feat of sounding like both Jay Z and Mick Jagger. Then the verses break into that glorious Motown-referencing chorus and the song takes off to a different dimension. The arrangement is multi-layered, taking in elements of cabaret, jazz, soul and Motown. If it had dropped on his desk in 1968, Berry Gordy would have been very, very happy. The song is also a triumphant lover's overcoming of being dumped, of love not working out. It's positive, a song about dusting down after heartache, a song that says yes we're over, but I'm not going to mope any more. The months of shuffling about like a ghost are over; in its place, a determination to get on with life.

Track eight, 'Wake Up Alone', begins like The Rolling Stones doing doo-wop. Pretty guitar, a musical box rhythm section. Lyrically, it's a lovely, open portrait of love gone wrong, Amy turning herself inside out and hanging her feelings out for all to relate to. It's music as diary,

Amy in a polka dot dress with her trademark slightly askew beehive hair-do. (ROSS HALFIN/IDOLS)

Amy shows off her Blake tattoo above her left breast, May 15, 2005. (SNAPIX)

Amy with Tyler James, September 8, 2005. (TIM WHITBY/WIREIMAGE.COM)

With boyfriend Alex Claire, in Camden, September 26, 2006. (BIGPICTURESPHOTO.COM)

Amy with her father Mitch Winehouse, at the Q magazine awards, London, October 30, 2006. (BRIAN RASIC/REX FEATURES)

Jools Holland accompanies Amy on his late night BBC2 TV rock show, *Later With Jools Holland*, November 3, 2006. (ANDRE CSILLAG/REX FEATURES)

Amy's record producer, Mark Ronson. (LFI)

Performing at Joe's Pub in New York, January 16, 2007. (JOHN RICARD/FILMMAGIC/GETTY IMAGES)

On the set of the 'Back To Black' video, London, February 6, 2007. (BIGPICTURESPHOTO.COM)

Amy with Alex Claire at the Brit awards,
London, February 14, 2007. (LFI)

Getting up to collect her Brit award, with
manager Raye Cosbert of Metropolis Music.
Amy's mother Janis is on the right.
(JM ENTERNATIONAL/REDFERNS)

A pint in either hand at the Dublin Castle for the Camden Crawl, April 19, 2007. (STUART NICHOLLS/RETNA)

Amy on stage at Coachella Music Festival,
California, April 27, 2007.
(JOHNSHEARER/WIREIMAGE.COM)

Amy's husband, Blake Fielder-Civil.,
photographed in April 2007. (REX FEATURES)

With Kate Moss at launch of her Topshop range in New York, May 8, 2007.
(MARION CURTIS/REX FEATURES)

Amy with Blake at the Isle of Wight Festival, June 9, 2007. (JON FURNISS/WIREIMAGE.COM)

Amy duets with Mick Jagger when she joined The Rolling Stones on stage at the Isle of Wight festival, June 10, 2007.
(DAVE HOGAN/STAFF/GETTY IMAGES)

At MTV Europe awards in Munch, Germany, November 1, 2007. (STAFF/GETTY IMAGES)

Amy's mother Janis. (REX FEATURES)

Amy's manager Raye Cosbert and her father Mitch arrive at Amy's house on the day of her husband Blake's court appearance, November 9, 2007.
(MARIO PIETRANGELI/SEAN PARSONS/BIGPICTURESPHOTO.COM)

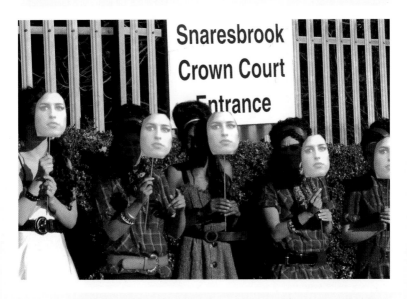

Fans with 'Amy' facemasks gather at Snaresbrook Crown Court as Amy W arrives to watch husband Blake being remanded, November 23, 2007. (STUART WILSON/STRINGER/GETTY IMAGES)

Amy checks out an early edition of her biography. (XPOSUREPHOTOS.COM)

music as journal, music as memoir. Again, the spectre of the relationship with Blake floats through the song, as Amy sings herself back together again.

'Some Unholy War' almost opens like an Otis Redding song (what a tease) before it steps straight out and away into a jazzy guitar figure, subsequently drifting about checking reggae, soul, Motown, doo-wop, making up an A to Z sketch of musical references. More than any other track on the album, it takes Amy into Lauryn Hill, Macy Gray, Erykah Badu territory, the drums shading Carribbean-flavoured pop.

'He Can Only Hold Her', opening with that sublime Motown shuffle, beautiful guitar, drum, piano, bass, would not sound out of place on a Smokey Robinson album. Then Amy's voice comes in, smoky, smoochy and expressive, like Diana Ross after a carton of Marlboro cigarettes. It's sunny, skipping, music as joy. The vocal phrasings are incredible, words bent and warped and punctured and chopped up, as Amy sings her lyric, deconstructing the words as she goes, until they mean exactly what she wants them to mean.

The album closes with 'Addicted', which kicks off like Miles Davis, then dives into that nagging Motown drumbeat. A tale of weed and love, it's Amy singing one of her particular urban love stories. It's an interesting track musically, a mash-up of traditional jazz, soul and Motown, Amy doing one of the things she does best, blending different musical genres from the past while singing a lyric very much specific to today, and in a vocal style that is timeless.

Chapter Eight

Straight To The Top

Island released 'Rehab' as the first single from *Back To Black* on October 23, 2006. Everything was different. The cover, a confident shot of Amy in a white raincoat, heels, long flowing hair, carrying a suitcase down a flight of stairs while surrounded by musicians, was entirely American in its imagery, its suggestions, its character. Gone was the girl-next-doorness of the *Frank*-era covers. The single was released in two formats – one backed with 'Do Me Good', the other with 'Close To The Front' and a remix of 'Rehab'. The single finally made good on all Amy's potential and entered the UK singles chart at number 19 on download sales alone, before shooting up the rankings when the CD was released, eventually peaking at number seven. The label had its long-hoped-for hit single.

It had been a gamble like many others in pop music. Three years on from her debut album and with a new sound, a far cry from the new-jazz soundscapes of *Frank*, would Amy Winehouse still be relevant? Pop moves fast. And what mattered in October 2003 wouldn't necessarily still matter in October 2006. As Amy returned, the Top 10 featured hits by the likes of Razorlight, My Chemical Romance, Girls Aloud, James Morrison and American camp disco revivalists The

Scissor Sisters. It was a different landscape to that of October 2003, when Dido and Norah Jones were blocking up the chart. But as soon as 'Rehab' ripped out of the starting gate, it was clear that Amy mattered more now than she had three years earlier.

To affirm her new-found celebrity, *Back To Black* hit record shops a week later, on October 30, and copies started flying off the shelves. The cover shows a dramatically thinner Amy sat before a blackboard on a wooden school-classroom chair. Illegible scribblings and drawings have been all but wiped off the board. She wears a dress, leopard-print heels, her hair is long and flowing, and two chunky necklaces hang around her neck. Staring into the camera, the look on her face is somewhere between critically vulnerable and extremely confident.

Her tattoos (which had shot up in number since *Frank* came out) were now a key element of Amy's look. In mid-2007, she confessed to having a dozen, including one in memory of her beloved grandmother, Cynthia (a heavy-duty Tony Bennett fan). She got her first, a Betty Boop tattoo on her back, when she was 15. She told *Rolling Stone* that when her parents found out about that tattoo, they "pretty much realised that I would do whatever I wanted, and that was it, really".

The album shifted over 40,000 copies in its first week of being on sale in the UK and looked likely to usurp *Frank* in every respect, and quickly too. A further 30,000 copies were sold in the second week, pushing the record straight into the album chart at number three. It would not stop there, eventually going all the way to number one.

Reviews were breathless. For *The Times*, "*Back To Black* is another record redolent with the tang of modern bohemia, building on the platinum-selling *Frank*'s witty exploration of sex and self-realisation." *The Guardian* called it "a 21st-century soul classic… starting with the pungent single 'Rehab', everything is in its right place: the exuberant neo-Motown swing supplied by producers Mark Ronson and Salaam Remi; the rich, sinewy vocals, somewhere between Lauryn Hill, Beth Gibbons and Etta James and the thoroughly modern songwriting, in which infidelity is betrayed by a telltale carpet burn ('You Know I'm No Good') and a lover is less desirable than a good supply of weed ('Addicted')."

The Observer had this to say:"Heralded as a starkly confessional album, it's a surprise to find *Back To Black* as chiffon-light in parts as it is unflinching in others. No one could accuse her voice of lacking light and shade either, tarrying as it does behind the beat on 'Rehab', reduced to a muttered husk on 'Tears Dry On Their Own', syrupy on 'Love Is A Losing Game'. Classicism is only half the story here. The chief delight of this record comes when Winehouse, a thoroughly Noughties kind of girl, scurfs off the patina of age with her forthrightness."

The *Jewish Chronicle's* review introduced Amy as a woman "with tattoos", who "swears like a docker" and "smokes weed". After checking the new-jazz roots of *Frank* and how that album had come to land her in a peer group alongside Norah Jones, Katie Melua and Jamie Cullum, the writer swiftly cuts to the chase, identifying just how different a record *Back To Black* was from *Frank*. Describing Amy as sounding "even more like a scorned 43-year-old black American woman", the review went on to say that the singer's "rafter shaking vocals belie her age, postcode, everything". Identifying the songs as being steeped in "blue mood balladry and neo Motown soul", the review concluded that Amy had once more proved herself to be "a startingly gifted artist".

The Daily Telegraph had this to say: "*Back To Black* sees a triumphant Winehouse slamming the door on those laid-back lounge influences and strutting into a gloriously ballsy, bell-ringing, bottle-swigging, doo-wop territory. Think wall-of-sound bombast with brazenly catchy hooks and smart, modern, soul-scouring lyrics. Think Ronnie Spector, Etta James, Edith Piaf and Marlene Shaw. Women whose favourite men are bartenders."

In short, the reviews were unanimously positive and appeared to collectively herald the album as an instant classic. The warm response added to Amy's already buoyant mood. She was in love again and had been dating Alex Jones-Donelly (sometimes also referred to as Alex Claire), a former Radio 1 executive turned chef since June 2006. The relationship would last for nine months, stretching into 2007, before she'd leave Jones-Donelly in March of that year to return to Blake Fielder-Civil. In photographs, he looks very much the nostalgic Camden ska fan – short blonde hair, jeans, Fifties zip-up jacket with a tartan lining, what looks like a Fred Perry shirt on underneath – the kind of individual who'd always turn out for a Madness reunion concert.

In July 2005, Jones-Donelly had been recruited from Radio 1 to join EMI Music Publishing – reporting to Guy Moot – as Senior Vice President, A&R. That meant him leaving his job at Radio 1 where he was Head of Music and Live Music. Moot was in charge of Amy's publishing deal at EMI, which probably accounts for how she and Jones-Donelly got together in the first place. The latter had started at Radio 1 in 1997, working as a music scheduler, before going on to become Head Of Music in 2000. In June 2004, he was promoted to the job he was doing when EMI head-hunted him. Prior to working at Radio 1, he had been employed at Kiss FM for seven years. He had also worked in a record shop, where his speciality was dealing 12″ dance singles; at the MCPS, where he also specialised in covering dance music, and on top of that, he'd also run a club night. At Radio 1, his main achievements included developing the station's live music output and giving a push to the careers of artists such as The Streets, Joss Stone, Dizzee Rascal, Franz Ferdinand, The Killers and Coldplay.

At the time of *Back To Black*, Amy, led by her relationship with Jones-Donelly, was in good spirits and good shape, having moved beyond the hellish period of depression that had followed her break-up with Fielder-Civil, not only by writing about it but, more superficially, by joining a gym. Amy told *The Observer* how she had given up smoking weed and instead become a gym junkie.

"The papers go on about how I lost weight but I didn't even notice myself losing it. I used to smoke £200 worth of weed a week, that's two ounces, which is disgusting, and it made me eat crap food on impulse. I lost the weight when I stopped smoking weed and got into the gym instead. I like my gym because there are all these sweaty men around to gear me up and get my adrenaline going. You want to sweat and look good. When I'm in a women's gym and they see me in my standard make-up (it's my war-paint, I wear it all the time), the women look at you as if to say, 'Who are you trying to impress?' At the men's gym it's like, 'Run girl, run!' I don't mind being looked at by men, I'm competitive."

Contradicting this new healthy image, Amy then made a disastrous, allegedly drunken, appearance on singer Charlotte Church's TV chat show, which aired on Friday, October 13. *The Jewish Chronicle* ran a story on the performance at the end of October 2006 under the headline "Putting the Wine into Winehouse". According to the paper, "Amy reportedly had trouble reading the autocue and kept shoving her head into the camera when it was focusing on other guests. She smashed her foot into a glass table as she stood up and later kept forgetting the words to a rendition of Michael Jackson's 'Beat It', which she sang with Church."

It's widely acknowledged that Church and Amy's duet on Jackson's 'Beat It' was white-knuckle TV of the highest calibre. While the classically trained Church actually sings the song, Amy fluffs the lyric and generally goes about singing the pop classic like a karaoke have-a-go in a provincial pub on a Friday night. It's train-wreck TV, the song lurching from one hesitant moment to the next, the viewer given the impression that it is perpetually on the verge of collapse. Contactmusic later reported Church as saying of the duet, "Amy kept forgetting the words. I told her, 'When I squeeze you, it's your turn to sing.' We did it with me poking her in the back."

The Daily Mirror covered the story under the headline: 'Amy Wino – Singer Drunk Charlotte Church TV chat show'. They then reported: "It takes a lot to upstage earthy Charlotte Church and veteran hellraiser Keith Allen. But Amy Winehouse managed to do just that with her shambolic appearance on the Welsh star's chat show. The smokey-voiced singer was, ahem, 'tired and emotional' at a recording of the *The Charlotte Church Show* on Wednesday. She seemed pretty together when introduced to the audience at the London Studios, on the South Bank, but it wasn't long before the liquid refreshments from the hospitality green room started to take effect. Amy began slurring her words and stumbling through a short piece to camera." The paper reported that in order to shoot the 'Beat It' duet, it was necessary to film three takes.

Days later, *The Daily Mirror* reported that Amy's label had advised her to tone down her drinking. The paper revealed what had gone on the day Amy taped *The Charlotte Church Show*, "We can reveal she'd guzzled champagne for breakfast and had a liquid lunch of vodka, whisky, Baileys and liqueurs. She also hit the bar in the green room at the TV show." The report then went on to discuss the label's concern that Amy's public reputation as a drinker was starting to become a problem. They quoted an insider as saying: "Amy is a vibrant character and the record company love the fact that she's got spirit, but her consumption of alcohol is seriously getting out of hand. She's turning up to interviews out of her head and she usually sinks more booze while being grilled about her life. We're all worried that she's going off the rails. She's been told that if she doesn't curb things she will have to go into rehab to sort herself out."

The *Mirror* also reported that Amy had confessed to "having an eating disorder". It quoted Amy as saying, "I went through every eating disorder you can have. A little bit of anorexia, a little bit of bulimia. I'm not totally OK now but I don't think any woman is."

Speaking exclusively to *The Daily Mirror* at the end of October, she talked again of the role clinical depression had played in her short life to date and how rehab wasn't for her. "I had to go to rehab to find out what it was like but it's not for me. It would only increase my anxieties. I was always prone to depression but I didn't realise how much. I was on anti-depressants and the pill when I was younger, but the hormones go crazy and it drove me mad. Creative people shouldn't be on anti-depressants or any drugs."

Amy's drastic weight loss between albums had already gone under the microscope in an article in *The Daily Mail* over the summer. The paper had reported on her gym attendance, explaining that after an initial free consultation with a trainer at Fitness First, a women's only gym in Chalk Farm, she had knuckled down to a strict workout regime. The article stated that Amy would do a full cardio, fat-burner workout and then move on to repetitions for toning, using the gym's various weights machines. The report said that she went six days a week to the gym, always between four and six in the afternoon. Quoting a source, the paper speculated that the media attention that went with *Frank* had made Amy self-conscious about image issues. "While she doesn't mind people criticising her music, she was devastated when snide remarks about her appearance were made."

The Sun reported in December how Amy had told Entertainmentwise.com about her battles with eating disorders, quoting her as telling the website, "I've had a flirtation with every eating disorder there is, I wouldn't tie myself down to one, and then I realise that I have to eat and I will fatten myself up and put on half a stone in a week because I'm good like that."

Meanwhile, to flag up *Back To Black*'s new sound and image, Amy relaunched her official website, www.amywinehouse.co.uk, as part of the marketing of her new look. She now had a new hairstyle too – a stacked-up beehive, worn in homage to the girl groups, in particular Ronnie Spector of The Ronettes. If you compare pictures of Spector during The Ronettes' heyday and pictures of Amy once she adopted this look, the hairstyles are identical. Amy later spoke of the beehive growing in proportion to how insecure she felt. Hair as protection, something to hide behind. Image as safety net.

In terms of getting the album out on the road, a crucial part of the campaign to catapult Amy to superstar status, a serious UK tour was announced for November. These dates followed three headline shows that she'd already played in September as a tease before the release of 'Rehab'.

The first of those three shows took place on September 10 at The Fleece in Bristol. *The Telegraph* reviewed the show, saying, "Overall, the music is still less interesting than Winehouse herself. She's funny and chatty. Her speaking voice is a one-woman production of *Little Britain*: the garbled haste of Vicky Pollard, the camp bark of Marjorie Dawes and the slightly unhinged gusto of that woman Matt Lucas plays who's always screeching, 'E's gawwwgeous!' The review then made a mandatory reference to her new image and significant weight loss: "She's even more striking than before: the caricaturishly huge mouth, Cleopatra eye make-up and eyrie of black hair are now perched atop a near absurdly minute body and foal's legs. Her skinniness has been pored over, inevitably, in celebrity magazines. It's certainly improbable that a frame so spindly should house a singing voice so colossal. At any rate, she goes down well, and not just with that yelping admirer at the start."

The Independent also reviewed the show, setting her the following context, "It's not enough to be a pop star nowadays – you have to be a victim, too. Amy Winehouse, the 22-year-old Jewish Londoner with the smoky voice of a mature African-American jazz singer, has gone from being a curvy teen to, reportedly, an emaciated fitness addict." The paper went on to say, "She messes up from time to time, but shrugs it off nonchalantly and humorously."

The next show, at the Concorde 2 venue in Brighton on September 11, was reviewed by local publication *The Argus*, whose reviewer was not impressed. "Tonight her performance was slack and failed to move. As song after song passed by without her ever giving more than 65 per cent, disappointment and frustration set in. Her band were good and at times groovy but there was a sense even they were waiting for things to kick off. The new songs showed much promise with less jazzy inflections and more ska and funky, doo-wop influences fighting their way through. But Amy never harnessed her own talent. She seemed self-consciously disembodied from her old songs and fluffed her lyrics more than a couple of times. With her boyfriend in the audience, perhaps she was feeling shy or perhaps she has grown out of her boy done me wrong shtick."

The Guardian was at her third show, at the Bloomsbury Ballroom in London, on September 12, to assess how *Back To Black's* supersize vintage sound came over live. This review also focused on her weight loss and on the guessing game that forthcoming single 'Rehab' surely was: "Winehouse's issues are the fulcrum of her music and the emotions they provoke seep into her smoke-stained voice. This is her selling point – her ability to evoke life as a London bohemian who stumbles across the wrong guy and to do it in a jazzy context. The difference, three years after *Frank*, is that she has acquired subtlety. Once upon a time, she belted. Tonight, cocooned by a cool brass section and male backing singers, she caresses." The review then went on to highlight the elements of the new Amy: "The first half of the set is a string of dreamy jazz-blues confections. The second half, where new songs are debuted, is hotter and curvier. The fuckery of Mr Jones is denounced on the swinging 'Me & Mr Jones', and on the exuberant 'Back To Black' she advises a philanderer to return to his girlfriend. Her voice rises to a gladiatorial roar, and the girls in the place yelp back. She's tiny but mighty."

On October 30, Amy was the centre of another controversy when she attended Q magazine's annual awards ceremony. During a speech by U2's Bono, who was collecting the Band of Bands award, she heckled the politically passionate Irishman, shouting, "Shut up! I don't give a fuck!" It was a moment where Amy's candour crossed the line into impropriety. Whatever anyone may have felt about Bono and his speech, he holds an iconic place in rock'n'roll history, and the moment played awkwardly: a very young artist, promoting only her second album, with everything to prove, heckling the respected frontman of one of the biggest bands in the world. Some cringed on her behalf, feeling she'd committed a rock'n'roll faux pas of the highest order. Others thought her outburst hilarious, were delighted someone had had the balls to confront Bono's political zeal and pronounce it of no interest whatsoever. Whichever way you looked at it, her label and management must have realised the potential for her outspoken persona to backfire at some point.

A sure sign that her music was striking a mainstream audience occurred at the turn of November, when reports broke that Amy was under consideration by the producers of the next James Bond film, then known only as *Bond 22*, to write and record the main theme. It was another key indicator that she had made a giant popular leap from *Frank* to *Back To Black*, tapped into a mass market and, as a result, was bound for large-scale success.

Chasing that earlier teasing trio of headline shows in September, she then embarked on a 10-date UK tour, opening at the Liverpool Academy 2 on November 10 before moving to the Leeds Wardrobe on November 11, Glasgow's Oran Mor venue on November 12, then arriving in London on November 14, when she performed at Koko.

To promote the Glasgow date, Amy gave a very candid interview to *Scotland On Sunday*. The reporter established the context: "Three years on from *Frank*, after a blink and you'd miss it spell in rehab, coping with an eating disorder and a break-up that she says made her want to kill herself, Winehouse's comeback is far from squeaky clean."

The reporter then mentioned Amy's increasingly scrutinised antics in the public eye. "When she appeared on *The Charlotte Church Show* recently, Winehouse was so inebriated that her finale with Church, singing Michael Jackson's 'Beat It', was completely incomprehensible. When I mention this though, expecting at least a touch of hungover shame, she just laughs and tells me she can't wait to see it."

Amy then goes on to say with typical candid aplomb, "I'm just a young girl who gets fucked up sometimes. Sometimes my head is screwed on tighter than bolts, but a lot of the time I do mess up and lose the plot like everyone does. But because I'm so defensive and sensitive I lash out a lot. I'm not a nice drunk."

Pressed to comment on the 'Rehab' story, Amy told the paper, "I really think if you have problems and you can't sort them out yourself you're in trouble anyway. I also got sent to food rehab, and that was exactly the same as the alcohol one. I walked in and was like, 'I don't need this', and walked straight back out. I had to tell myself, 'Amy, you're not the queen of the world and you don't know everything.'"

She also talked of cracks in her relationship with Jones-Donelly. She told the paper that they lived together in Muswell Hill, north London, sharing a house with friends and that for her, things had plateaued. "Our relationship has become very domesticated and there's no romance any more, no fireworks. But I'll make it work with him because I love him so much."

When the tour reached London, *NME* was there to review the Koko show, saying of Amy's onstage persona, "She's like a wide-girl Queen Mum, sipping chardonnay on a heart-warming cockney meet and greet during the blitz, except the only bombs dropping in this venue tonight are soul-packed musical ones. Oh and the Queen Mum never looked like a cross between Ronnie Spector and an award-winning tattooed lady from Coney Island."

On November 16 she appeared at the Birmingham Academy 2, on November 17 at the Manchester Academy 2 and then at the Norwich Waterfront on November 18. Amy apparently got into an exchange of words with a member of the audience at the Waterfront, as reported by the *Norwich Evening News*: "The star, as famous for her alleged alcohol-induced antics as her popular bluesy melodies, was asked to leave the area after being involved in a confrontation with a male reveller following her gig at the Waterfront last Saturday." The paper then quoted a spokesperson for the UEA bar: "At the Meltdown Disco after the concert finished Ms Winehouse was socialising. She took exception to a comment made by a young male and had a confrontation with him because she was annoyed. There was a bit of a fracas. The door staff did what they are trained to do. The young man was led away and Ms Winehouse was asked to leave the area."

On November 16, the BBC screened Amy's appearance on the legendary pop quiz show *Never Mind The Buzzcocks*. Like her appearance on *The Charlotte Church Show*, it sparked widespread debate. (Amy had been on the show before, appearing in an episode hosted by Mark Lamarr that went out in March 2004.) Amy joined fellow guests Andrew Maxwell, Alex Pennie and Penny Smith, and was introduced by host Simon Amstell as an "Ivor Novello-winning jazz Jew". Amy appeared as part of Bill Bailey's team, going against Phill Jupitus' side.

Early in the show, Amy asked Amstell for a drink. He told her that she could not have one, saying, "Already a bit tipsy, Amy." He then says, "You want us to sit here, while you drink yourself to death." He then asks her if she's aspiring to be like Pete Doherty, and she says she's going to meet him later, to discuss their duet. Amstell then warns her off meeting Doherty and instead suggests she go and see Katie Melua, her old fellow BRIT alumni. Amy replies: "I've rather have cats Aids, thank you."

During one moment, Amstell thanks Amy for being on the show and says it's part of a new BBC remit, to have "more Jews, less carbon emissions". At one point, Amy spits onto the floor and Amstell playfully objects, saying: "You come here, full of crack, spitting all over things." Amy replies: "Let it die please." And Amstell says: "The addiction, I'd like to die. I want you back. This isn't even a pop quiz any more, it's an intervention, Amy."

Amy's appearance was irreverent, playful, charismatic, yet more train-wreck TV, and led some to draw comparisons with similarly on-the-edge drunken TV appearances by hell-raising actor Oliver Reed. Compared with her previous appearance, when she had come across as shy and retiring, here was the new *Back To Black* Amy, larger than life, giving off the vibe of one in the middle of a complicated tightrope walk. She seemed both very sure of herself and precariously insecure. Her hair and tattoos seemed to offer protection, a wall to hide behind. As TV it was entertaining and mischievous, endearing Amy to viewers who enjoy guests who are provocative and unruly.

Throughout the show, as Amstell alluded to Amy's newfound status as tabloid darling, his comments tapped into the mystery of why she had attended a rehab centre in the first place. His references to addiction, crack and alcohol, not to mention the line about the intervention, seemed to fall awkwardly. The intrigue surrounding her habits was reaching boiling point, and Amstell describing her as being "already a bit tipsy" when she asked for a drink, reflected growing concern about whether she was overdoing the partying. If the Amy Winehouse of *Frank*, appearing on the show in 2004, had come across as shy, polite, then this Amy, complete with spitting on camera, seemed like rock'n'roll trouble. This appearance played up the image the tabloids were creating for her, and sealed her reputation as an increasingly unpredictable and outrageous wild card.

On November 24, a story on her appearance appeared in *The Jewish Chronicle*, homing in on the Jewish mischief between Amy and Amstell. Part of the article read: "The piece de resistance was the lyric round in which, rather than asking Amy to come up with the words to a Led Zeppelin or Supremes number, as is traditional on the show, nice Jewish boy Amstell decided to test Winehouse on her knowledge of Hebrew folk music. Shamefully she failed completely to come up with the next line to *Hava Negila* and it was left to Amstell to inform her in beautifully accented Hebrew, that the answer was *venismechah*."

In the meantime, the tour moved on to the Cambridge Junction on November 10 and, on November 21, she returned to Bristol, to perform at the Carling Academy. On November 24, she concluded the 10-date tour by appearing at the Little Noise Sessions, Acoustic At The Union season at the Union Chapel in London's Islington, alongside Mika and Bat For Lashes. The season, curated by Jo Whiley, was a fundraiser for the learning disability charity Mencap.

At the beginning of December, *The Irish Times* ran an interview with Amy, who was again enthusing about the girl groups who inspired elements of *Back To Black*. She told the paper what she specifically liked about each of the groups dearest to her: "The Shangri-Las, very dramatic and atmospheric. The Ronettes, very stylish. The Shirelles, they had coolness and attitude, they had vulnerability." She then elaborated about what it was that she liked so much about this music: "I loved those heartbreak songs they used to do, especially the way the girls sounded so heavenly. Yet they were also singing about the kind of heartbreak you would find at the bottom of a bottle of whiskey. They knew all about sorrow."

She also reflected on the changes in her personal life, discussing again her transition from weed-smoking chanteuse to fit gym devotee: "I don't smoke weed anymore so I'm not so defensive as I was back then. I'm not as insecure as I was either. I go to the gym, I run loads and I'm much healthier than I was."

She also looked back on the making of *Frank* and admitted that she had not been in control of the sound as much as she would have liked. "When you have a producer with you who is far more experienced, you do tend to become a bit, 'yeah, that's cool', in the studio and go with the flow. And when you're smoking weed, you just don't care about anything except who has the next joint."

She also told the paper that the album had thrown up various issues in terms of marketing. "It was my first album and I didn't know what I was doing so I was learning as I went along. I don't think the label had a clue what to do with it either, so it was a learning curve for them as well."

The interview offered insights into her relationship with Jones-Donelly. She talked of him as a calming influence, a stabilising force in her life. This is borne out in photographs of the couple from the time in which Jones-Donelly is pictured carrying Amy's bag – he took care of her. Despite all the talk of jogging and going to the gym, Amy did admit that she still loved a drink. "I do drink a lot and I'm a bad drunk, a very violent drunk. It's only since I started going out with my boyfriend Alex that I have realised what a horrible drunk I am. My ex-boyfriend would be saying things like, 'stop doing that, you're an idiot' and rowing with me when I was drunk, which just made me worse. With Alex, he will bring it up the following day when I've sobered up. It really embarrasses me to hear I've punched him in the face six times. Of course, it does make me want to cut down on the booze. I really do try not to drink, but I'm a very self-destructive person."

The paper followed up the interview a fortnight later with a year-end round-up, which lamented, "Amy Winehouse received much attention in 2006, sadly as much for her drinking as for her powerful *Back To Black* album. It's a pity, because the album is as sassy and sharp as they come, Winehouse hitting the basement with the soul sisters for the best wannabe Motown album of the 21st century."

NME then reported that Amy was planning on cutting a track with Babyshambles' Pete Doherty – something Amy had mentioned as being on the cards on *Never Mind The Buzzcocks*. The report mentioned that Doherty had wanted them to duet on a Billie Holiday cover, but Amy had not been keen on the idea. It quoted her as telling BBC Radio Six, "I was like, 'no, let's write something together'. I like writing songs, he's an amazing songwriter and I'd love to say that I wrote a song with Pete Doherty."

She saw out the year by appearing on Jools Holland's annual *Hootenanny*, which went out live on TV. Amy performed a version of Marvin Gaye's 'I Heard It Through The Grapevine' with Paul Weller, then sang a cover of Toots & The Maytals' 'Monkey Man'.

It had been a whirlwind end to the year, an autumn of extremes as Amy was swept away by a rush of enthusiasm for *Back To Black* bigger than anyone might have expected or hoped for. Her various controversial moments – *The Charlotte Church Show*, *Never Mind The Buzzcocks*, heckling Bono at the Q Awards – had amplified the buzz that started with 'Rehab' and turned her into a bug under a media microscope. That song asked the listener: Is the narrator of this song, ie. Amy Winehouse, in need of treatment for alcohol dependence or, worse, alcoholism?

In interviews promoting the album, she laughed her rehab episode off, saying it was absurd, that she had gone along to meet the addiction counsellor purely to appease her former management. She reiterated that she was old-school, believed in a person sorting their own issues and problems out by their own means. She did not believe in the concept of a rehab centre, nor did she believe that she had needed to go to one for a consultation in the first place. In her mind, it was all nonsense. She'd been in an intense relationship that combusted, the heartbreak had caused her to become depressed, and the two in tandem led her to drown her sorrows using alcohol. She'd ended up writing an album about that painful era, moved on, met a new man, dumped the weed habit, started going to the gym and dropped a few dress sizes, end of story.

And yet those controversial public appearances suggested all was not fine, that she was actually standing on the ledge, vulnerable in the glare of escalating fame and notoriety. Or was she simply having fun with all the attention? Goofing about, the way countless artists before her had goofed about when pushed into the spotlight at a rapid speed?

Hadn't Nirvana's Kurt Cobain taken to fame by swearing and, toppling amp stacks on TV shows, and generally lashing out against a media that suddenly courted his attentions so insanely after 'Smells Like Teen Spirit' and *Nevermind* stormed the charts? Wasn't Amy just falling into a pop/rock fame cliché by taking to the spotlight with a combination of glee and terror? Was she comfortable with all the attention or thoroughly uncomfortable with it all?

Regardless of what was going on, she ended 2006 safe in the knowledge that her career was in a purple patch. *Back To Black* was to be released in the US – a clear message from her label that she had broken out commercially on the grandest of scales. At home it was selling feverishly and sitting at number two on the UK album chart. And then there she was, on New Year's Eve, live on television, singing with Paul Weller, and it was about the music again, only the sweet music, not the circus of Amy Winehouse, young woman with issues who wears her heart on her sleeve. That was how things should have been. Music, first. Artist, second. But the balance was under threat. In the coming year, the music would increasingly lose the battle as the priority in terms of public interest.

Chapter Nine

This Year's Kisses

The city was New York of course. Where else for Amy Winehouse to charge the United States? Los Angeles would be too soft, too mesmerised by a celebrity guest list. Chicago wouldn't quite suggest that her label believed it was were dropping the biggest star in British pop music onto the American public. Atlanta or New Orleans would be too low-key. Seattle still wears the stamp of grunge, no good therefore for an artist peddling a record like *Back To Black*. Miami would speak too explicitly of a bid to woo the dance crowd, the club scene, and would set Amy up for remixes and dance-floor stardom. The goal was total national domination, from East Coast to West. If *Back To Black* had the potential all involved felt it had, there was no reason why Amy couldn't take the entire American music market and turn it on its head. To achieve that goal, of course they'd launch the charge in New York City.

The scene of Amy's arrival on American soil was a deliberately modest venue in Manhattan called Joe's Pub. The smallness of the venue and the discretion of the booking were signs of marketing genius. In a venue of that size, there was no way demand for tickets and guest-list places could ever be met. Once word got out that Amy was coming, it was like pouring an ocean into a thimble, which was exactly what the strategy was designed to do. *Back To Black* had an American release date now – March 13 2007. The date allowed the album to snowball in the UK and Europe, work up a feverish hype. By the time it hit American stores, it would have been out in the UK for nearly five months. In that time, word of mouth about *Back To Black* would inflame the American media network, creating huge demand for it. In terms of releasing the record, Island/Universal had sold the album to Universal Republic in the US.

The 160-seat Joe's Pub, part of the Public Theater, sits in the East Village at 425 Lafayette Street, between Astor Place and East 4th Street. Since 1998, the club had staged countless shows by artists such as Alicia Keys, Eartha Kitt, Bebel Gilberto and Norah Jones, and that lineage set the scene nicely for Amy's US debut on Tuesday January 16, 2007. She arrived in the US on a high. At home, *Back To Black* had hit the number one spot on the UK album chart. She could not have landed in the US at a better moment or with a bigger success story. The show sold out so fast that the venue added a second appearance on the same day, at 11pm. She took to the stage backed by The Dap-Kings, who had of course performed many of the songs on *Back To Black* so beautifully with their vintage soul infatuations.

Back home, Amy had a second single out from *Back To Black* – 'You Know I'm No Good'. Released on January 5, 2007, it again featured a strong cover, consistent with the graphic identity of *Back To Black*. One CD single featured a head shot of a contemplative Amy reclining in a bath tub. Another featured her sitting on a wall wearing a green and white dress, defiant and challenging. Aimed at the American market, another version of the single featured a remix of 'You Know I'm No Good' by Wu-Tang Clan's Ghostface Killah. Other tracks across the various formats included a live take on 'To Know Him Is To Love Him' and a cover of Amy's live staple, Toots & The Maytals' 'Monkey Man'.

Her association with a hip-hip heavyweight like Ghostface Killah gave her impeccably good credentials for a run at the American market. And it was good for her reputation at home, too. While the cringeworthy appearances on *The Charlotte Church Show* and *Never*

Mind The Buzzcocks had dented her image, the remix of her track by Ghostface Killah, complete with his trademark husky rapping, reset the dials on her cool factor. Born in Staten Island, New York, in 1970, the rapper had been involved with the seminal Wu-Tang Clan recordings as well as multiple solo albums like the acclaimed *Supreme Clientele*. In the UK, the single would end up peaking at number 18, nearly a dozen places lower than its predecessor, 'Rehab'.

In the crowd at Joe's Pub was an impressive array of distinguished guests, including Jay Z, Mark Ronson, Dr John, Alice Smith and Mos Def. According to a review in *Spin* magazine, Amy "took to the stage dressed like a quintessential Bond Girl of the Connery era" and wowed the audience with "her seductive croon and impressive vocal acrobatics". *Village Voice* described her entrance this way: "Backed by a taut 10-piece band, she hit the tiny stage like a tatted-up Ronette from hell, complete with thick black eyeliner, fabulously ratted bouffant weave, and a skintight, strapless cocktail dress."

Entertainment Weekly noted: "In the UK, Amy Winehouse is a pop star and tabloid regular due to her outrageous behavior, reported eating disorders, and performances where she appears to be very, very drunk. The bold-faced rappers didn't just come for spectacle, however. Sure, Winehouse keeps gossip columnists busy, but her New York coming-out proved she's much more than mere shtick."

Even British tabloid *The Daily Mail* had a reporter on the scene, who wrote of the show: "Despite showing some nerves, Amy won over the crowd, which included rappers Jay-Z and Mos Def, with her jazz-infused vocals perfectly backed by her tight funk band. It seems that reports that Ms Winehouse, who has been nominated for two BRIT Awards, is in dire need of rehab after being forced to quit a show after one song due to feeling 'tired and emotional', judged by this brilliant performance, are premature."

The morning after the show, news reached Amy from home about those BRIT nominations: the British Female Solo Artist award, for which she would go head to head with Corinne Bailey Rae, Jamelia, Lily Allen and Nerina Pallot, and also the Mastercard British Album award, in competition with Arctic Monkeys, Snow Patrol, Lily Allen and Muse.

The Joe's Pub shows helped calm down the storm following her disastrous performance at the G.A.Y. club night at London's Astoria venue on Saturday, January 7. That was the show *The Daily Mail* was alluding to when Amy had to abandon her performance after just one number. Apparently, she had come out on stage, struggled through the song and then headed backstage. According to a report the following day in *The Sun*, "She fled after just one song and I hear it was Kelly Osbourne's fault as the pair had been out boozing all day. Furious fans are now demanding refunds. One told me, Amy managed one song quite well, then legged it. The organiser came out and said Amy was throwing up and to bear with her. But she never came back. Everyone was booing." Two months later, Amy told Canadian publication Chart Attack what happened that night and blamed everything on jet lag: "I had to get off a plane, go and have a laugh with my friend, be silly, have a drink and then go do that show. And obviously I couldn't."

While in New York she did an interview with *The Washington Post*, during which she told its reporter that certain aspects of her personal life, certain issues, had been exaggerated by the media. The reporter relayed Amy's thoughts as follows: "Winehouse says of various published reports about her alleged bulimia, anorexia and bipolar disorder, 'It got blown out of proportion'. She does say that she suffers from depression, and that she's not the most secure person in the world. But then, she says, neither is any other musician she knows." The article also theorised about Amy's success, quoting Bill Bragin, the former director of Joe's Pub, as saying, "She's got a great voice; she's got great songs, she's already coming with a larger than life persona. She's got all the elements of a star. She's got the talent, but she's got something that gets her into Perez Hilton when she doesn't even have an album in the US. She's the real deal."

Celebrity blogger Perez Hilton (www.perezhilton.com) had indeed been writing prolifically about Amy and affording her the same wittily written blog inches as celebrities such as Britney Spears, Victoria Beckham and Jennifer Aniston. The comments attributed to Bill Bragin were spot on. Here was a British artist who was yet to have a single record released in the US and yet her personal life was already a source of fascination in certain American circles. Her notoriety in the British tabloids had travelled across the internet and become a phenomenon. Her antics since the release of *Back To Black* had played out like a chaotic soap opera, and people were fascinated, hooked on the unfolding saga.

The Washington Post article ended with Amy arriving late for a photo shoot. The reporter notes, "She's shy and she's shaking. She stutters as she talks and searches for words, her eyes welling with tears. Her left arm is abraded and raw. Something caused the injury, but she isn't sure what. 'I got drunk and I don't remember.'"

Back home, she embarked on another UK tour, once more ticking off the key cities. The first show was at the Cambridge Corn Exchange on February 1, then she took a fortnight's leave before continuing at the Southampton Guildhall on February 18, transferring to Wales to take in Cardiff University on February 19 and then visiting the Midlands for a show at the Birmingham Academy on February 21. On February 23, she played the Liverpool Academy, two days later the Manchester Academy and then, on February 26, the tour bus visited the campus of Northumbria University. After that, on February 27, she played the Glasgow Academy before taking a hiatus. The tour continued on March 3 at the Sheffield Octagon, moving on to Nottingham Rock City on March 5 before climaxing with a two-nighter, on March 8 and 9, at the Shepherd's Bush Empire in London. Now big enough to sell out two nights at a venue that size in London, Amy must have been pleased at how fast her popularity was growing.

In the middle of the tour, on February 14, the BRIT Awards ceremony was held at London's Earl's Court arena. It was a great night for Amy – she won the Best Female Solo Artist award, knocking back stiff competition. Her acceptance speech was very simple – she said she was glad her parents were in the audience. The award officially confirmed how popular she was becoming and seemed to underscore what the media attention and record sales (*Back To Black* had by now shifted 500,000 copies in the UK and was sitting tight at number one on the UK album chart) were already saying, which was that there was now no bigger British female artist in the UK.

She also appeared at the *Elle* Style Awards in February, turning up with her new friend, Kelly Osbourne, celeb daughter of rocker Ozzie and his high-profile wife Sharon. *The Evening Standard*'s website posted photographs taken of Amy at the awards that led to speculation that she was self-harming. "She was seen at the *Elle* Style Awards earlier this year with red marks, cuts and scratches on her arms. The singer claimed afterwards that she had taken a drunken tumble during an alcohol-induced blackout in New York."

The photograph of Amy and Kelly was captioned, "Amy Winehouse with Kelly Osbourne: In this picture taken recently, evidence of Amy's self-harming is clearly visible." *The Daily Mail* also noted that the *Elle* Style Awards had sparked concern and speculation, "Pictures which emerged of her arm criss-crossed with scars sparked rumours that she may have been harming herself."

The UK dates did not run smoothly and Amy ended up cancelling both shows at the Shepherd's Bush Empire. A spokesperson informed the media that the dates were to be rescheduled for May 28 and 29. Amy ended up having to make a public apology to one pair of fans who had tickets for the March 8 show – Elton John and David Furnish. Her apology went as follows, "Sorry about that (Elton). There'll be a next time."

One possible explanation for the cancellations that did the rounds was that Amy had lost a tooth. She later told MTV that it happened after she bit down on an ice cube and afterwards felt the tooth wobbling around, apparently having come loose from the gum. She asked her boyfriend, Alex Jones-Donelly, to pull it out for her, but he wouldn't. Eventually, she told the network, she tugged at it herself until the tooth came completely loose and fell out. Thereafter, as many newspapers and magazines noted, she sported a gap in her teeth.

Behind the scenes, Amy's relationship with Jones-Donelly had come to an end after nine months. She was devastated by the break-up and increasingly exhausted by her work schedule. Speaking after the cancellation of the London shows, her father Mitch Winehouse told *The Sunday Mirror*, "I'm not ruling out rehab. Amy needs a break. They don't send you to rehab just because you've broken up with someone. There are other things. Amy needs a rest. Her workload is absolutely manic. She's an emotional girl. Her schedule has caused problems with Alex. He wants to see her. I don't know if that's the reason for the break-up but wouldn't you want to see your boyfriend now and again?"

In mid-March, Amy went back out to the US to follow up that incendiary double-show at Joe's Pub with a mini-tour of low-key clubs in support of the American release of *Back To Black*. She would play at the Bowery Ballroom and make a high profile appearance on *Later With David Letterman* (performing 'Rehab'), both on March 13. She then moved on to perform at the Universal Republic Showcase at the SXSW festival in Austin, Texas, on March 15, and at the Island UK BBQ event at the same festival the next day, before flying out to the West Coast to play two shows in Los Angeles – the Roxy Theater on March 19 and Spaceland, out in the trendy Silverlake neighbourhood, on March 20. In the case of venues like Spaceland, the label was keeping it as low-key as possible, relying on the hype that had spilled over, as intended, from the Joe's Pub shows. But the Spaceland show wasn't to be. After performing to a crowd at the Roxy Theater that included Bruce Willis, Courtney Love and Fabrizio Moretti from The Strokes, Amy ended up cancelling the Spaceland date. *NME* reported, "It is rumoured that Winehouse believes the venue is too small to accommodate her large band."

By the time she'd wrapped in Los Angeles, news reached Amy that *Back To Black* had crashed into the US album chart at number seven, selling 50,000 copies in its first week of release alone. The entry position set a record – never before had a British female solo artist had a record enter the US album chart that high. (Ironically, Joss Stone would outdo Amy one week later.) The label must have been delighted, especially since Amy's debut album had been held back from US release, but that was already in the process of being changed. Republic was working on a plan to release *Frank* in the US later in the year. Tapping into her stateside success, the heavily influential *Rolling Stone* featured her in a 10 Artists To Watch special, introducing her to readers with the following extremely funny equation: "(Aretha Franklin × Janis Joplin) – Food = Amy Winehouse".

There was excitement on the relationship front too, when late in April Amy announced that she was engaged to Blake Fielder-Civil – the former boyfriend who broke her heart and inspired many of the songs on *Back To Black*. This was the boyfriend with whom she had suffered a disastrous relationship in 2005 that had sent her spiralling into depression when it ended, and yet here she was, a month after splitting up with Alex Jones-Donelly, not only dating Fielder-Civil again but was making plans to marry him. What's more, according to *The Sunday Mirror*, there was talk of her fiance converting to Judaism so the couple could have a Jewish wedding during the summer. According to *The Sun*, Fielder-Civil had proposed to Amy on April 23 at her flat in Camden, where the couple were living. Amy deliberated over his proposal for 24 hours before saying yes. Fielder-Civil then pulled out a diamond ring from Tiffany & Co.

Meanwhile, Amy was in the US yet again, playing further dates. She made an incendiary appearance at the Coachella Festival on April 24, then played at Popscene in San Francisco on April 26, the Empire Polo Grounds in Indio, California on April 27, and then at the Fox Theater in Boulder, Colorado, on April 30.

The same day as the Boulder gig, Island released the title track from *Back To Black* as a third single from the album in the UK. Backed with a cover of The Specials' 'Hey Little Rich Girl' and a rendition of The Zutons' 'Valerie' (later to feature on Mark Ronson's *Version* covers album), the single reached a UK chart high of 25, considerably lower than either 'Rehab' or 'You Know I'm No Good'. The cover of the single showed a slick Amy sitting in an armchair with a blonde streak in her hair, looking upwards as if at a wall-mounted TV or the sky.

Meanwhile, the US dates continued, taking in the Varsity Theater in Minneapolis on May 2, the Schubas venue in Chicago on May 3, the Theater Of The Living Arts in Philadelphia on May 6, the Paradise Rock Club in Boston on May 7 and the Highline Ballroom in New York on May 8 and 9. The tour closed with a pair of dates at the Mod Club in Toronto on May 12 and 13.

Once the tour wrapped, Amy and Fielder-Civil flew down to Miami, where speculation mounted that they were going to tie the knot. Amy declined to comment, but there was a palpable sense that something was about to happen. And then it did, and in typically irreverent Winehouse fashion she and Fielder-Civil married at a private ceremony at the Miami-Dade County Marriage License Bureau in Florida on May 18. The rumour mill went berserk until Amy's American publicist confirmed that yes, the couple had married. She and Blake then spent a couple of days honeymooning at the Shore Club hotel, on Miami's South Beach, which was designed by British architect David Chipperfield.

On May 24, the 52nd Ivor Novello Awards ceremony was held at the Grosvenor House hotel in central London. Amy had been nominated in the Best Contemporary Song category for 'Rehab'. She was up against Hot Chip for 'Over & Over' and Bodyrox for 'Yeah Yeah'. On the night, Amy was triumphant, as she had been at the 2004 awards.

The Daily Mail then reported that Amy and Fielder-Civil were to have a second wedding, in north London, so their families could participate. Amy told the paper, "I'm so glad I got married to Blake, we've been in love for such a long time but we didn't realise it until lately. People have been talking about me having a Jewish wedding, but I'm not interested in that, that's bullshit. We are just going to have a nice family party to celebrate in December." The paper reported that the Florida wedding set the couple back approximately £60 and that afterwards they went for a "wedding breakfast of hamburger and chips". The report also stated that, "Her parents Mitchell, a taxi driver, and Janice, a pharmacist, found out about it in the newspapers." Amy told *The Daily Mail* how they took it: "My dad was all right about it really, it was more my mum that wasn't. I would have loved my family to have been there but it was something just for us."

Amy then went back to work after the honeymoon, playing the two rescheduled Shepherd's Bush Empire shows at the end of May. *The Daily Mail* reported her as telling the crowd, "Don't know if you heard but I just got married to the best man in the entire world." They then watched as she blew kisses to her husband, who was in the balcony.

On Saturday June 9, Amy appeared on the main stage at the Isle Of Wight Festival, sharing a bill with Muse, Donovan and Kasabian. She played a strong set, including 'Rehab', her cover of The Zutons' 'Valerie', 'You Know I'm No Good', 'Cherry' and 'Love Is A Losing Game'. The next day, June 10, The Rolling Stones headlined the main stage and invited Amy to join them for a searing cover of The Temptations' soul classic 'Ain't Too Proud To Beg'.

Six days later, the latest edition of *Rolling Stone* hit the news-stands, with Amy on the cover. It was the surest sign that she had arrived in the US as a mainstream artist. With intimate photographs by Max Vadukul, the in-depth article, which ran under the headline 'The Diva And Her Demons', noted Amy's rapid ascent to American fame, mentioning that rap icon Jay Z had recently remixed 'Rehab' and that Prince was now doing a mean version of 'Love Is A Losing Game'. The article, citing the *Never Mind The Buzzcocks* appearance and the Bono heckling incident, went on to quote Mark Ronson as saying of her wild behaviour, "Amy is bringing a rebellious rock 'n' roll spirit back to popular music."

Rolling Stone's correspondent managed to snatch a typically candid interview from Amy and was not afraid to ask the difficult questions. Like this, for instance, tackling the subject of Amy's alleged self-harm: "I point to my left forearm and say I couldn't help but notice the scars. How old were you when you started doing that? She looks at me surprised, but doesn't have a ready-made answer, so I continue, I mean the cutting. Her muscles seem to tighten and she avoids eye contact as she replies, Um that's really old. Really old. Just from a bad time I suppose. And then, stammering, D-d-desperate times." The mention of the stammer suggests that such moments in interviews were becoming increasingly difficult for Amy. Having presented herself as unflinchingly candid when *Frank* came out, it was hard for her now to turn around and take the opposite approach to interview. So people asked intimate questions, expecting intimate answers.

Spin magazine also put Amy on the cover of its July issue, emphasising the circulation battle between the two powerful American music magazines. The cover shot – of Amy in a leopard-skin print dress, with the straps fallen from her shoulders to expose Blake's pocket tattoo over her heart – underlined the Amy paradox: the photograph made her look simultaneously vulnerable and yet very sure of herself. The shot was taken by Terry Richardson, the celebrated photographer and stylistic descendent of gritty realists such as Larry Clark and Nan Goldin. Born in New York in 1965, Richardson was known for his cutting-edge work as much as for his celebrity portraits, and bringing him in to shoot Amy was *Spin*'s way of playing up the risqué elements of her public image, simultaneously underscoring that while her records had mainstream pop appeal, she was no manufactured pop star.

Richardson shot her with his trademark raw sensuality. Watching the footage of the shoot at Spin.com, you see a man scoping his subject from every conceivable angle and perspective. It's the method of an artist whose work has appealed to fashion magazines, style magazines, fashion-brand advertising campaigns and art collectors alike. He first came to attention in the mid Nineties, and *The Observer* wrote that his reputation grew from his knack of "shooting fashion editorials and ads that were starkly lit, brutally cropped and shot on snapshot cameras with little or no lighting."

In the website footage, as Richardson crouches, attentive, snapping away with his camera, Amy stands up against the white wall in denim shorts and a black bra, wielding a shard of broken mirror. She then allegedly carved "I Love Blake" across her stomach, very lightly but with immense concentration. From the footage archived at Spin.com and shot by Blake, it seems Amy is in a kind of trance. It matches accounts of the dissociative state of the self -harmer. Richardson carries on working, even though you can sense he's distracted by what his subject is doing.

The papers back home jumped on the story. On Wednesday June 27, for instance, *London Lite* reported the incident under the headline 'Wild Winehouse stuns fans with self-harm stunt during interview'. The paper said, "Winehouse, who is suspected of self-harming, posed for a photo holding a piece of broken mirror for rock magazine *Spin*. Minutes later, she pulled up her top and carved I Love Blake into her skin."

The *Spin* article, run under the cover headline of 'Up All Night With Amy Winehouse', opened with a series of context-setting questions: "Sixties retread of pop's most original voice? Hardcore rebel or misunderstood tabloid target? The second coming of Aretha or of Courtney?" The questions, which introduced the cover story, were laid out next to a colour photograph of Amy laughing hysterically, practically nose to nose with a rooster.

The piece caught the phenomenon of her recent success full on, stating, "Three years ago she was an innocuous, girl next doorish virtually tat-free, full-figured, neo-jazz crooner with middling sales and no American distribution – now she's Sid Vicious." The article showed Amy to be baffled by her achievement, caught in the glare of it all. She told *Spin*, "I don't care about any of this and I don't have much of an opinion of myself. I don't think people care about me and I'm not in this to be a fucking role model. I made an album I'm very proud of and that's about it. I don't think I'm such an amazing person who needs to be written about."

On June 22, Amy appeared at the Glastonbury Festival in a surprisingly low-key, mid-afternoon slot on the opening day. *The Guardian* reviewed the show, saying, "Though Winehouse's live voice is flawless, she bares more than a passing resemblance to a rabbit caught in the headlights. It takes a few songs to shake off the nerves, but she never quite loses the slightly traumatised expression." Amy then moved on to play at other festivals – at Hove on June 26, Les Eurockéenes de Belfort in France on June 29 and the Rock Werchter festival in Belgium on June 30. Trouble then emerged just before she was due to play the Summer Pops concert series in Liverpool on July 4 and the T In The Park festival in Kinross, Scotland, on July 7.

In the case of the Liverpool show, Amy cancelled 15 minutes before she was due on stage, disappointing 4,500 fans. A spokesman said she had pulled the show on the orders of a doctor who had visited her backstage. Then, an announcement went out about T In The Park. Her management issued a statement reading, "Amy Winehouse has unfortunately had to cancel her appearance at T In The Park due to exhaustion. Following a year of non-stop touring and promotion, Amy has been advised by a doctor to take time off and rest. Amy would like to apologise to fans for this cancellation."

She then also cancelled her July 8 appearance at the Oxegen festival in Dublin and her July 13 turn at the Nuke festival in Austria, again citing exhaustion. Speculation ran wild about what was wrong with her. Exhaustion arising from overwork? Was she pregnant? Burned out from partying too hard? A serious illness?

Amy returned to the road to honour her July 17 show at the Eden Project in Cornwall, but, according to a review in *The Daily Mail*, she was still showing the strains of a frantic year. "Reports say Amy appeared to be in tears while onstage, hitting herself on the head with a microphone in frustration when she forgot the words to her songs, and a fan said she finished by spitting into the crowd. The shambling performance ended when she stormed offstage during her last song, a cover of 'Valerie' by The Zutons." A spokesperson for Amy told the media that the show offered no reason for concern: "Amy was annoyed with herself. She is a bit ring-rusty after not having played for a while and was upset after making a few mistakes in the set."

The next night, Amy returned to Liverpool to play a rescheduled performance of the cancelled July 4 date. BBC Liverpool reviewed the show, opening with the matter of the earlier cancellation. "They say honesty is the best policy. So Amy Winehouse gained a bit of respect at her rescheduled Summer Pops gig in saying, 'Thanks for having me back after I bottled out.'" Of the show, the reviewer wrote, "You couldn't help but be astounded by the sheer power of her voice, which seemed to emanate effortlessly from her tiny lungs no matter which jazzy-soul song from latest album *Back To Black* she was performing."

Amy then picked up her summer schedule, performing at Somerset House in central London on July 20 and then at the Benicassim Festival in Spain on July 22. On July 25, she played a terrific but tiny show at the Institute of Contemporary Arts in London. A review of the date appeared in *The Daily Mail*: "At the ICA last night, as part of the ongoing iTunes festival, the 23-year-old provided a spectacular reminder of exactly why she was declared best British female artist at this year's BRIT Awards and why she is the bookies' favourite to scoop this year's coveted Mercury Music Prize. Winehouse appeared on stage 50 minutes late, flanked by a nine-piece band decked out in slick black suits that were in keeping with the soulful Sixties vibe of her acclaimed album, *Back To Black*. Her tiny physique, clad in a black and white vintage dress, the straps of which fell down repeatedly throughout the show, Winehouse achieved instant forgiveness for her poor timekeeping as soon as she opened her mouth. 'Tears Dry On Their Own', which made good use of the band's brass section, showed off Winehouse's breathtaking voice. Live, even more so than on CD, Winehouse's voice was truly soulful."

On August 5, Amy turned in an outstanding performance at the Lollapalooza festival in Chicago. And then, on the brink of playing at the Oya festival in Norway on August 8, she again had to cancel the show. Her band had just finished soundchecking when the message reached them that Amy was not well. There was some word about her having been treated at the University College London hospital. The cancellation came as news reached Amy that she had received three nominations for the MTV Video Music Awards. Nobody knew what was going on. They assumed she had gone down with exhaustion again and had cancelled on doctor's orders.

The real reason for her being unable to appear in Norway was far more serious, and would soon revealed the full extent of the stress and strain that her spiralling fame and success had inflicted upon her.

Chapter Ten

Girl At Her Volcano

With help from a female friend, Blake dragged Amy through the doors to the A&E department at University College Hospital in central London. It was 1am on August 7, 2007. They half-carried her to the reception. Then, according to a report in *The Sun*, "Her legs buckled and she fell to the floor with a shriek." Nurses rushed her through to the treatment area. The emergency team immediately took over and gave her an adrenaline shot, then pumped her stomach. Her head was reeling with the news of her three nominations across three categories in the MTV Video Music Awards, but the promise of another accolade was soon lost inside this crisis.

The medical team stabilised her, settled her. The record company was informed. The following day her performance at the Oya festival in Norway was cancelled. The crew were already there, the band too. All that day, as Blake came and went from Amy's private room in the hospital, rumours began flying about the star's collapse. *The Sun* reported that Amy had previously "admitted using marijuana and cocaine" and had been "boozing heavily", and also highlighted prior comments by Amy regarding alleged eating disorders: "I have had problems with my weight. Everyone was going on about it being caused by cocaine but it wasn't a drugs thing. I was somewhere between being bulimic and anorexic. It was triggered by splitting up with my last boyfriend. I was doing a few drugs but only dabbling. Cocaine isn't really my thing and I was never really on it."

On August 9, the story hit the tabloids. Here it was: the seed sown with the 'Rehab' single blown to gory enormity. A major clue had just been provided for the ongoing guessing game about her health. Was Amy Winehouse partying too hard? Here was the answer. A hospital emergency. A near tragedy. Celebrity gone off the rails. *The Sun* put the story on its front page under the headline 'Wild Pop Star Has Adrenaline Jab And Stomach Pumped: Amy In Drugs Collapse'. Their report read, "Amy Winehouse was dragged through an A&E unit's double doors before collapsing from a huge drug overdose yesterday. The party-loving star's trademark beehive hair hung lank around her shoulders as staff at London's University College Hospital rushed her for emergency treatment. Tattooed Amy, whose stick-thin frame and sallow complexion have worried friends and fans alike, was given an adrenaline shot in the early hours drama. And she had her stomach pumped."

That same day, *London Lite* ran the same story under the headline 'Amy Ready For Rehab: Singer may go into clinic after suspected overdose'. The paper speculated that Amy was "seriously considering" checking into a treatment programme after her "suspected overdose" in the early hours of Monday night/Tuesday morning. The paper quoted a "close friend" who had said, "Amy got a massive fright when she was hospitalised and is finally coming round to everybody's pleadings with her to go to rehab. She now realises she may need help as her lifestyle finally takes its toll."

The following day, Friday August 10, *London Lite* reported that Amy had entered The Priory rehab centre in Roehampton: "Amy Winehouse has checked herself into rehab following a suspected drugs overdose. The troubled singer was treated in hospital after collapsing on Wednesday. She is seeking help at The Priory in Roehampton after her shocking drink and drugs lifestyle finally took its toll."

The same day, *The Sun* featured a more in-depth report of the story behind the hospitalisation, again putting it on the front page, this time under the headline 'Amy's 3-Day Binge: Coke, Ecstasy, Horse tran-quilliser, Vodka, Whisky'. The story inside explained how a sleep-deprived Amy had been drinking all day at various pubs. She had arrived back at London's Heathrow airport from Chicago, where she'd performed at Lollapalooza. From the airport, the partying started at the Robert Inn in Hounslow, where Amy drank vodka and lemonade and Blake downed pints of lager. A local told *The Sun* that Amy and Blake played pool and that the couple made "repeated vis-its to the toilets".

They apparently left the pub around 3pm. Next stop was the Hawley Arms in Camden. There, a fan told *The Sun*, he'd seen Amy drinking Jack Daniel's. Then, she and Blake threw a party at their Camden maisonette. *The Sun* quoted a friend of Blake's as saying: "It was like she had pressed the self-destruct button. She was downing coke, pills and ketamine, vodka and Jack Daniel's."

The friend also told *The Sun* how Amy had at one point picked up a pink guitar and started strumming and singing, only to abandon the song and start sobbing. Another friend told *The Sun* that Amy had been telling everyone that she hadn't slept for three days. Then she started convulsing. Blake called friends. When she didn't come round, it was clear they needed to get her to the A&E. Her father visited her in hos-pital. Then, when doctors gave her the all-clear, she was discharged and left the hospital by a rear exit.

It was after this that her label announced to the press that Amy was suffering from "nervous exhaustion". *The Sun* report also mentioned that Amy had become enamoured with the poetry and decadent leg-end of Lord Byron, and believed she had little time left to live.

On August 11, *The Sun* ran another story under the headline: 'Amy Winehouse – I'm Suicidal', which reported on further aspects of the hospital drama: "I can also disclose the disturbing development that the star had been smoking heroin on the night she overdosed. Contrary to reports, Amy, who collapsed this week following a three-day drug and booze binge, is desperately ill." The article said Amy had been staying at the Four Seasons Hotel in Hook, Hampshire, since leaving hospital. It said of her state of health, "She has been unable to eat and has been vomiting non-stop. She has been visited by doctors and a psychiatrist is due to see her today. Last night a family friend said, 'Amy has told her mum she is often suicidal and she knows she will die young.'"

On Tuesday August 14, *London Lite* carried a story about Amy under the headline 'Amy: I am On Hard Drugs But Can Beat Them'. The article stated, "The singer, who collapsed last week after taking a cocktail of heroin, ecstasy, cocaine and the horse tranquilliser ketamine is now in rehab in the US." The report stated: "He (Blake) and Winehouse, 23, both denied injecting heroin." The article claimed the couple had been in rehab in the US for three days.

A day later, *The Daily Mirror* ran with a story headlined 'Star's Mum In Law Talks'. The article reported that Amy had made a confession to her parents-in-law days after the collapse about hers and Blake's drug use. Revealing details of the "confession", the paper stated, "She and Blake, 25, are being treated together for heroin and cocaine addiction at a secret location in America." Days earlier, the paper alleged Amy had come clean to her in-laws about what had been going on. Blake's mother Georgette told the paper, "It's the hardest thing in the world for me to say in public that my son and his wife have a drug problem. They've admitted it." Georgette also told the reporter, "I know my son's had a drug problem ever since he was 20 and moved down to London." The article followed the family dramas of the previous weekend.

After the collapse and hospitalisation, Amy and Blake had, according to *The Daily Mirror,* seen a Harley Street GP and agreed to a referral at a rehabilitation centre. The trip to Harley Street followed a family summit on August 10 at the Four Seasons Hotel in Hook, where Blake and Amy's parents met the couple for a showdown about the events of the previous week. It was there, over Ovaltine and chocolate cake, that Amy told Georgette how things really were. "She told me she was addicted to heroin and cocaine," Georgette relayed to the paper.

That night, Amy's in-laws went to bed, sure that Amy's confession spelled an imminent end to the terrifying events of recent days. But during the night, according to *The Daily Mirror*, Blake and Amy picked up heroin from a dealer and smoked it in their room. They were found out by Juliette Ashby. According to the paper, Ashby saw "charred pieces of foil" in Amy's suite in the morning and told Amy and Blake's parents. At breakfast, Amy denied Juliette's allegations. Mitch apparently became angry and blamed Blake. Then, when Blake's father defended his son, Mitch was incensed. Giles Civil told *The Daily Mirror:* "He was getting highly emotional and kept blaming Blake for Amy's problems." The report continued by saying that Amy, seeing her father so upset, felt compelled to confess to everyone present that she and Blake were addicted to drugs. Georgette then took the initiative and called the Harley Street GP, who came to the hotel and began making arrangements that would see the couple transferred at the earliest opportunity to a treatment centre in the US.

Contradicting stories that the couple were in rehab in the US, on the next day, August 16, *The Sun* ran a front-page photograph of Amy and Blake under the headline, 'Amy Quits Essex Rehab'. The accompanying report stated that Amy and Blake had left a rehab programme at the Causeway Clinic in Essex the day before – the day after *The Daily Mirror* carried the comments from Amy's mother-in-law.

The report said that Amy had checked out of the centre after less than 48 hours, having been admitted with Blake on Monday August 13, despite family calls that they seek independent treatment. She and Blake took a helicopter back to Camden. They then went for a check-up with a GP on Harley Street, presumably the same doctor who had been called to the hotel by Georgette. A source told *The Sun*, "She wanted to leave on Tuesday evening. People close to her are devastated. But Blake wants her to return to normality – and we all know what their normality is." The article then alleged that Mitch had looked into getting a restraining order taken out on Blake, believing it would give Amy a better chance of coming to her senses regarding her drug and alcohol abuse and get help.

In the middle of the drama, Island released a new single from *Back To Black* – 'Tears Dry On Their Own', backed with 'You're Wondering Now' and various different mixes of the main song. The single would end up peaking at number 16 in the UK.

London Lite ran a story on Thursday, August 16, under the headline 'Amy's out of rehab… and straight back in a pub'. The paper said that

Amy and Blake, having returned to Camden from the Causeway Clinic, were out that night with Amy's in-laws at Camden pub, the Old Eagle. The story quoted Giles Civil as saying: "We were praying they wouldn't bail out early. We don't want them to go back into their vicious cycle."

In the meantime, Amy cancelled her appearances at the V Festival in Staffordshire on August 19 and at the Rock en Seine festival on August 25. And then, much as fans feared, news broke on August 22 that Amy had now cancelled her entire forthcoming US tour, slated to start on September 12 in New York. Her publicist said she had been ordered to rest by medical professionals and therefore had no choice but to reschedule her US dates for early 2008.

The cancellations were extensive, with Amy having many dates booked for September, including several outdoor festivals as well as prestigious theatres coast to coast. The shows were intended to further boost her profile in the US; without them all her hard work to date could potentially count for nought. But her health was at severe risk and, for this reason, the promise of further success and sales had to be put on hold.

Then, just when things seemed as though they couldn't get any worse, on the morning of Friday August 24, stories appeared about a bust-up at the Sanderson hotel on Berners Street in central London. Amy and Blake had apparently had a shocking fight in their £500-a-night room at the luxury hotel in the early hours of the night of Thursday August 23.

According to *The Daily Mail*, Amy came out of the hotel alone at around 11pm and went to meet another young woman in the street. She reportedly hugged her, then went back into the hotel. The *Daily Mail* report continued: "The singer returned to her hotel room and within hours other guests complained of raised voices, clattering furniture and screaming. Shortly afterwards, the concierge was called. Miss Winehouse, who has a history of self-harming, had asked for medical assistance to patch up cuts on her arm."

The report then cited the accounts of other guests who said that around 2.30am on Thursday morning, arguing between Amy and Blake reignited. Amy was then seen running down the hotel corridor to the lift, pursued by a "badly bleeding" Blake. *The Daily Mail* reported that a fellow guest witnessed the couple at this time: "One guest who got into the lift to reception at the same time said they started shouting at each other: 'Amy was in floods of tears. This guy was screaming at her. She was cowering in the corner and I thought he was going to hit her. When the lift door opened, she took off across the lobby at a real pace.'"

Around 3am, Amy and Blake both appeared in the hotel reception and she hurried out to the street, pursued once more by Blake. It was then that photographers noticed the state the couple were in. Amy flagged down a car and jumped in. The car sped off and dropped her close to Charing Cross station, where she bought cigarettes – Camel Lights – at a 24-hour shop. The couple then contacted one another by mobile phone and were reunited by 4am. They then went for a walk, seemingly having calmed down.

On Friday morning, *The Daily Star* put photographs of Amy and Blake on the front cover. Blake had criss-cross slash marks on his face and neck. Amy, her eye make-up running hopelessly, appeared to have a bloodshot eye and a scratch or cut near the brow. In their accompanying article, *The Daily Star* quoted an onlooker as saying that Blake looked like "the victim of a sustained knife attack". The alleged argument between Amy and Blake happened at the end of a long night. Blake was seen chasing Amy out of the hotel and up the street. Photographs of Amy showed her left wrist and arm bound with white plasters.

The Daily Star reported an onlooker as saying: "Amy hit a few bars and was knocking back strawberry daiquiris like there was no tomorrow. Then she was wandering through the streets looking like a sad cross between a homeless child and a bag lady." The report then stated that Blake chased after her, screaming her name. Instead of returning to her husband, she flagged down a car and jumped in.

Of the various photographs of the couple showing them bloodied and shocking, none captured the moment more poignantly than one of Amy's shoes – blood-soaked pink ballet pumps, tattered and stained. Here was a young woman stunned by fame walking straight into the flashes of the paparazzi, baring the wounds of celebrity fall-out on perfect pink ballet shoes designed for a graceful ballerina. The shoe photograph was an image of horror, disclosing painful secrets of what's going on in the life of the woman wearing them. All across London, those who bought tabloid newspapers were wondering to themselves, what's the matter here?

Once they'd sorted things out, the couple checked out of the Sanderson at 4am, Amy carrying her white handbag and their framed wedding photograph.

Showbiz columnist Perez Hilton reported the story in typical fashion on his renowned and highly entertaining blog. He wrote, "Fuck the fake Hollywood bullshit. Fuck the bullshit! Amy Winehouse is going to die if she continues down this destructive path!!!!!!! Click here for very graphic pictures of a bloody fight that erupted between Wino and her husband in the wee hours of Thursday morning. We do believe in God and we pray that he is able to help save Amy from death, which she keeps inviting into her life. And ditch that loser husband!!!!"

Then, on Friday morning, Hilton followed the story by sending Amy a text message. He then reported that she had replied, saying: "Blake is the best man in the world. We would never ever harm each other. Take back what you said on the blog. I thought you was my girl. I was cutting myself after he found me in our room about to do drugs with a call girl and rightly said I wasn't good enough for him. I lost it and he saved my life."

Amy then sent three further text messages to Hilton, one saying, "For the last time he did not and never has hurt me. Say I told you what happened on your blog. He has such a hard time and he so supportive. Please make amends. Kiss. Amy x." Hilton then reports that she sent one final message, which read: "Please can you put up the truthful version straight away? It's bad enough that it's been there that long. I know you love me but he deserves the truth, he is an amazing man who saved my life again and got cut badly for his troubles. All he gets is horrible stories printed about him and he just keeps quiet, but this is too much. Thanks girl. Amy."

The story took the Amy Winehouse public image to a new place. It sent shivers down spines, spoke of a personal life that was in tatters.

Gossip in the entertainment industry about substance abuse and drug overdoses is one thing. But photographs of a couple seemingly cutting each other up in the name of love signalled the point at which most people lost a rational connection to Amy Winehouse. Except maybe those touched by the horrors of self-harm, who took a step closer.

After those photographs went public, who didn't want to take her in, give her a hug, run her a hot bath, feed her something wholesome, make her a cup of tea, sit her down, wrap her in a blanket and say, "Now what's wrong?" Those images were not rock'n'roll or Hollywood. Those images were not fashion or TV. Those images were simply disturbing. They tested the boundaries of what we consider normal and threw Amy into a whole new category.

After the drama, Amy and Blake flew to the Caribbean, where they holidayed at the Jade Mountain resort on St Lucia, costing them up to £1,000 a night according to *London Lite*. While they were there, Mitch Winehouse made public remarks about how he felt having seen the photographs of his daughter after the night at the Sanderson hotel. *The Sun* reported him as saying, "It was sickening seeing those pictures. No, it was worse than sickening – I wanted to die." *The Sun* also reported comments from Giles Civil, who said of his son and daughter-in-law, "They are going through abject denial at the moment. They don't see themselves as having a problem and are quite aggressive in defence of themselves. They believe they are recreational drug users but it seems this is not the case and clearly they are addicts."

On August 29, *The Daily Mail* reported that Giles and Georgette Civil had publicly called for fans to boycott Amy's records and to stop playing her music, in a bid to "stop the singer and her husband from killing themselves with drugs". Of the Sanderson hotel incident, the paper said, "Her pink ballet pumps were stained in blood where she had allegedly injected heroin between her toes."

The same day, *Metro* carried the story of Amy's in-laws talking to the BBC's *Radio Five Live*. They quoted Giles Civil as saying: "There's only one way out of this and anyone with drug experience will tell you, the only way out is not sectioning them, not locking them up.

At some point they are going to reach rock bottom and at that point, they will say, I don't want to do that any more."

On August 30, *The Sun* ran a story that highlighted the despair Mitch Winehouse was going through over his daughter's personal struggles. "Every day," he told the paper. "I go to my father's grave and pray." The paper reported the reason for these prayers as follows: "Mitch, 57, believes only divine intervention can now stop drugs from killing the out of control singer." It continued, "In a thinly veiled attack on Blake, he claimed his daughter's severe self harming and drug addiction kicked off only shortly after their marriage three months ago."

The month ended with yet more bad news, an announcement that Amy would not be appearing as billed at the MTV Music Video Awards ceremony in Las Vegas on September 9. Once again, her health was given as the reason for the cancellation.

On September 4, back from St Lucia, Amy returned to the stage and, against all expectations, gave a stunning performance at the Mercury Music Prize ceremony at London's Grosvenor House Hotel, singing, 'Love Is A Losing Game' accompanied only by acoustic guitar. Amy's *Back To Black* album had earned her a nomination, and she was up against Arctic Monkeys, Bat For Lashes, Dizzee Rascal, The Klaxons, Maps, New Young Pony Club, Basquiat Strings With Seb Rochford, Fionn Regan, Jamie T, The View and The Young Knives. She didn't win – The Klaxons collected the prize for their *Myths Of The New Future* album and pocketed the £20,000 cheque – but she told *London Lite*: "I am really well at the moment, thanks. I had a great holiday with Blake and I really don't know what the fuss was about."

The day before the startling performance, the *London Paper* had covered her return to the UK. The news report touched on rumours about Amy's stay in St Lucia: "Pictures emerged this weekend that suggested Winehouse had been using heroin on holiday. She was also said to have been vomiting blood, suggesting serious illness, but refused to see her doctor."

On September 17, *London Lite* covered another story about Amy, reporting: "Amy appears to be back to her alarming self-harming ways. Yesterday, Amy, famous for her aptly named hit 'Rebab', was seen jumping out of a taxi in Chelsea shielding a nasty cut on her right hand. In fact, the injury was so bad that it soaked a hanky Amy was using as a makeshift bandage and even left blood splattered on her shoe." The report continued: "Along with drugs and eating disorders, Amy has been plagued by a self-harming tendency for some time."

The drama continued when she performed at the MOBO Awards on Wednesday September 19 at London's O2 Arena. *London Lite* made the show front page news the following day, with the headline: 'Amy's a wreck at the MOBOs'. Amy and band performed 'Tears Dry On Their Own' and 'Me & Mr Jones'. The band looked tense, on edge, as they chased Amy's unpredictable vocal performance around the stage. There was a feeling of a well-rehearsed band trying to figure out which cues from Amy to follow. She sang raw, wonderfully, then shambolically, as if suddenly losing control of the lyrics and the flow of the song. She looked unsure of herself, pinned beneath the spotlight, her magic unavailable. By the end of 'Me & Mr Jones', she seemed to be singing at a different rhythm to the band. *London Lite* quoted a bandmate, who wished to remain anonymous, as saying, "When she drinks it's the lesser of the two evils. At least she was just drunk. If she'd been on drugs tonight, things could have been a whole lot worse." *Metro* reported of the show: "She appeared distracted. She even appeared slightly out of time with the band at some points." It was another triumphant night for Amy though, as she picked up the Best UK Female award, beating Beverley Knight, Corinne Bailey Rae and Joss Stone. The same night, across town, Amy won another award – Best Female Performer – in the Vodafone Live Music Awards held at Earl's Court.

On October 8, Amy didn't even turn up to the Q Awards to collect her Best Album award. Instead, Mark Ronson received it on her behalf. *The Daily Mail* then reported that the award ended up in an unlikely location, "The gong was left at Bar Soho in London's Old Compton Street, where Mark Ronson, who earlier collected the award in her absence, was seen partying until 2am. But it is possible Amy's 'Valerie' duet partner was not entirely to blame, some reported last seeing the award in the hands of comedians Alan Carr and Ricky Gervais."

Most of October was mapped out with a planned European tour. She played at the Tempodrom in Berlin on October 15, the CCH 3 in Hamburg on October 16 and the Vega venue in Copenhagen, before heading into Norway on October 17 ahead of her date at the Peer Gynt venue in Bergen on Ocober 19. On her day off, October 18, she and Blake got into another scrape that was picked up by the media the next day. The couple were held in police cells in Bergen overnight, after, as *London Lite* reported, they were "arrested for drug possession". Apparently, police had stormed their room at the SAS Hotel Norge in Bergen at around 7pm on October 18, after "Hotel staff alerted police after smelling marijuana smoke coming from Winehouse's room." According to the article, they were released in the early hours of Friday 19 October and each fined £350 for marijuana possession.

The tour continued on October 20 at the Sentrum in Oslo and then moved on to Amsterdam, where Amy played the Heineken Music Hall on October 22. On October 24, she was at the Muffathalle in Munich, on October 25 the Volkshaus in Zurich and then at the Alcatraz in Milan on October 26. She then performed in Cologne, at the Palladium, on October 28, the Olympia in Paris on October 29 and at the AB Club in Brussels on October 30.

While in Germany, she gave a candid widely syndicated interview to the magazine *Stern*. *The Daily Mail* picked up on the interview and on October 25 quoted her as saying of her struggles with depression: "I feel that a black cloud hangs over me. I have taken pills for depression but they slowed me down. I believe there are lots of people who have these mood changes." The *Mail* then added, "This might also explain the singer's tendancy towards self-harm."

During those dates, Mark Ronson released his collaborative cover of The Zutons' 'Valerie', with vocals by Amy, as a single. The highlight of his *Version* album, which had been released back in April 2007, the single shot up to number two on the UK singles chart. The song showcases one of Amy's most remarkable vocals to date, a tremendous, soaring, off-the-cuff performance, full of amazing creative energy. Just listen to the way she sings the word "lawyer" – it's hairraising and magnificent.

On November 1, Amy appeared at the MTV Music Video Awards in Munich, performing 'Back To Black' and collecting the much-coveted Artist's Choice award. Four days later, there was new product: a deluxe edition of *Back To Black* was released in the UK, featuring a bonus CD of miscellaneous rare and live tracks. On the same day, Island released the live DVD *I Told You I Was Trouble: Live In London*, which included a concert film shot earlier in the year at one of the rescheduled Shepherd's Bush Empire dates and a brief documentary featuring interviews with Amy, Darcus Beese and Mitch Winehouse. Amy's father appears in the film working behind the wheel of his black cab, his job since leaving his prior career as a double-glazing salesman.

On November 9, 2007, *The Daily Mirror* published what it claimed to be a 'World Exclusive'. On the front cover, beneath the headline, 'Amy's man is cuffed and off to cells', was a photograph of Amy kissing Blake, her hands cupping his face, his hands bound behind his back in handcuffs, before police led him away for questioning. Beneath that, 'Winehouse husband held in trial fix sensation'. The report inside, by Stephen Moyes, described how Blake had been "sensationally arrested... over an alleged plot to fix a trial". The story continued, explaining how eight plain-clothes policemen arrested Blake as Amy looked on, her husband saying: "Baby I love you. Baby I'll be fine." The arrest, according to Moyes, took place at a flat in Bow, east London.

Earlier, the police had used a battering ram to break down the front door to Amy and Blake's flat in Camden. The arrest related to the upcoming trial on Monday, November 12 at which Blake and associate Michael Brown were set to appear accused of assaulting a bartender at the Macbeth pub in Hoxton, north London in June 2007.

On November 12, Amy was pictured despondent outside Pentonville Prison, having been refused permission to visit Blake. Only one visitor was allowed per week and they had to have put in a formal request 24 hours in advance. That visitor had been Blake's mother Georgette, who had put in the necessary advance request. Amy appeared pale, drawn and tired. The dramas of the year were taking their toll, one calamity after another having piled up on her skinny shoulders.

To maintain her sanity and out of respect for her fans, Amy launched her tour, regardless of the crisis over Blake's arrest and detainment. Many felt she would not be up to it, being far too upset at being separated from her husband. But still, she wanted to honour her commitments in a year when so many dates had been cancelled. But then, the night before the tour started, another drama unfolded. Apparently, according to a story in *London Lite* on November 14, Amy's parents called an ambulance to go out to the east London flat where Amy had been staying since Blake had been taken into custody. The ambulance arrived at the property at 7.30pm but no one was home. When the police arrived at 9pm, they found Amy, safe and sound. A source told *London Lite*, "Amy's family are petrified she'll do something stupid. They know she's very low at the moment and misses Blake terribly." When the family couldn't get hold of Amy they feared the worst and dialled 999. Despite this, Amy woke the following day and travelled up to Birmingham, ready to open the tour.

The first show was at the 13,000 capacity NIA venue in Birmingham on Wednesday November 14. Reports unanimously rated the show as a flop. *London Lite* splashed Amy on its front cover with the headline: 'Amy hits the lowest note as she lays into her fans'. The review reported how Amy, distraught at being separated from her husband, namechecked him throughout the show. The review mentioned how she came to the stage "totally out of it" an hour after the show was meant to begin and "proceeded to forget the words to her own songs". The details got worse: "She had trouble holding her guitar and dropped her mic numerous times. She even fell over at one stage." Eventually, fans tired of the unprofessional performance and some booed. Amy responded uncharacteristically, shouting: "Let me tell you something. First of all, if you're booing you're a mug for buying a ticket. Second, to all the people booing – just wait until my husband gets out." She then reportedly started crying and called the audience "monkey cunts". The headline to the *London Lite* review said it all: 'Awful Amy fires a four-letter drunken tirade at her loyal fans."

The BBC reported, "Amy Winehouse was booed by fans as she

delivered a shambolic set on the first night of her UK tour in Birmingham. During the show, the 24-year-old told the crowd, 'To them people booing, wait 'til my husband gets out of incarceration. And I mean that.'" The review then mentioned how, during an encore, when she was singing 'Valerie', "she stopped singing, dropped her microphone and walked off the stage."

The Times was slightly more lenient and had this to say: "Even by her normal soap-opera standards, this last fortnight has been unusually turbulent for Amy Winehouse. As the 24-year-old singer launched her biggest British tour to date in Birmingham last night, her headline-grabbing husband, Blake Fielder-Civil, languished behind bars on charges of attempting to pervert the course of justice in an assault trial. At the close of a tumultuous year of dramatic arrests, drug confessions, public fights and family strife, has life in the limelight tamed the rehab queen of British pop? No, no, no." The review mentioned concerns that Amy would not even show up for the first night of her tour, then noted that while she did turn up, she went on stage nearly an hour later than billed. The reviewer made comparisons between Amy and Pete Doherty, but highlighted differences as well, "Unlike Doherty, the North London siren appears to have gained extra career momentum from her backstage troubles, rather than being ravaged and hobbled by them. A few weeks before this sold-out tour began, her *Back To Black* album was confirmed as the biggest-selling British release of 2007." The reviewer then theorised, "It could be argued that Winehouse's bad-girl antics have added an extra dash of Edith Piaf-style authenticity to all those fabulously overcooked 1950's tramp-vamp lyrics about bruised hearts, toxic addictions, men behaving badly and women behaving worse." Despite this, the review was not positive: "The size of the venue also appeared to overwhelm her at times. The fetchingly sloppy, intimate delivery that works a treat in smaller clubs does not translate well to arenas and some of her bouncy retro-soul hits fell a little flat."

The tour moved on to Glasgow Barrowlands for two dates on November 16 and 17. The tour was then thrown into chaos by the resignation of her tour manager. *NME* ran with the story on November 16 under the headline 'Tabloid Hell: Amy Winehouse's tour manager quits over drugs'. The story, which originally appeared in *The Sun*, reported that Thom Stone had left her tour "after supposedly passively inhaling heroin that was on Winehouse's tourbus". *NME*, taking up the story from *The Sun*, relayed how the tabloid had reported that Stone had gone as far as taking medical tests to quantify if any heroin traces were in his bloodstream and the tests had come back positive. He had concluded that the only way heroin traces could be in his system were if he had inhaled the drug passively while riding the tour bus as a passenger. *The Sun* had apparently quoted a source who said: "Thom had just had it up to here. He was watching them (Winehouse and husband Blake Fielder-Civil) get off their heads and wondering whether Amy was even going to get up on stage. It was a nightmare job."

As if her haemorrhaging public reputation was not bad enough already, Amy was singled out for criticism by a senior UN official, Antonio Maria Costa, head of the United Nations Office on Drugs and Crime. He said Amy Winehouse and supermodel Kate Moss were "glamourising" cocaine use and warned that a growing interest in cocaine would only lead to Colombian drug barons carving more and more developed trafficking pathways into European cities. At a drug conference in Madrid days earlier, Costa had said: "Look at Kate Moss who still receives lucrative contracts after she was photographed sniffing. Rock stars, like Amy Winehouse, become popular by singing, I ain't going to rehab, even though she badly needed and eventually sought, treatment. A sniff here and a sniff there in Europe are causing another disaster in Africa, to add to its poverty, its mass unemployment and its pandemics." The story, as reported in *The Daily Telegraph*, highlighted as an example how the West African nation of Guinea-Bissau was heavily influenced by Colombian drug cartels that used it as a base, along with Ghana, Nigeria and Mauritania, from which to send drug mules to European destinations. The report also checked a new British Crime Survey showing that six per cent of 16-24 year olds had tried cocaine – making Britain, according to the *Telegraph*, the second biggest cocaine-using country in Europe after Spain.

To make matters worse, video footage of Amy in concert was posted on YouTube and heralded a new controversy. According to *The*

Amy Winehouse performs at the Riverside Studios in Hammersmith, London, for the 50th Grammy Awards ceremony via video link on February 10, 2008. (PETER MACDIARMID/GETTY IMAGES FOR NARAS)

Amy performing via video link on the Grammys. (RICHARD YOUNG/REX FEATURES)

Amy and family, brother Alex, mother Janis, aunt Melody Abelson (Mitch's sister), father Mitch and his wife Jane in back row after her Grammy performance at the Riverside Studios in London.
(RICHARD YOUNG/REX FEATURES)

Mark Ronson and Amy perform at The Brit Awards 2008 at Earls Court, February 20, 2008. (MARK ALLAN/WIREIMAGE)

The 46664 concert honouring Nelson Mandela's 90th birthday in London's Hyde Park, June 27, 2008. (RICHARD YOUNG/REX FEATURES)

Amy takes a sip of red wine during her performance at the travelling 'Rock In Rio' music festival in Arganda del Rey, Spain, July 4, 2008. (JUAN MEDINA/REUTERS/CORBIS)

Amy at the T In The Park festival at Balado, Kinross, Scotland, July 13, 2008.
(CENTRE PRESS AGENCY/REX FEATURES)

Amy performing on the main stage at the
V Festival, Weston Park in Staffordshire,
August 16, 2008. (KIRSTY UMBACK/CORBIS)

Amy's erratic appearance at the The End Of
Summer Ball, in London's Berkeley Square,
September 25, 2008. (RICHARD YOUNG/REX FEATURES)

Amy Winehouse lunges at a photographer as she leaves her Camden home, November 5, 2008.
(REX FEATURES)

Amy leaving Gaucho's, Dean Street, London, October 26, 2009. (BERETTA/SIMS/REX FEATURES)

Amy with boyfriend Reg Traviss at the opening of the Shaka Zulu restaurant, London, August 4, 2010. (REX FEATURES)

Amy with goddaughter Dionne Bromfield at the Q Awards, Grosvenor House Hotel, London, October 26, 2009.
(RICHARD YOUNG/REX FEATURES)

Amy on stage during her final concert at Belgrade in Serbia on June 18, 2011. After this performance, in which she appeared to slur the lyrics to her best-known hits, she cancelled the rest of her European tour.
(REX FEATURES)

Amy's last appearance on stage, at the Roundhouse, Camden Town, on July 20, 2011, with goddaughter Dionne Bromfield. Amy hugs Dionne before saying her goodbyes to the crowd and finally leaving the stage. (MARK ST GEORGE/REX FEATURES)

Left to right: Amy Winehouse's brother Alex, mother Janis, father Mitch Winehouse and ex-boyfriend Reg Traviss look over floral tributes outside Amy's Camden Square home, July 25, 2011. (SYLVIA LINARES/FILMMAGIC)

Flowers and tributes left by mourners outside Amy's home after her death on July 24, 2011.

(PAUL BROWN/REX FEATURES)

Amy at the Coachella Valley Music & Arts Festival at the Empire Polo Fields, in Indio, California, in 2007 (TIM MOSENFELDER/CORBIS)

London Paper, which made it front-page news under the headline 'Amy on the brink of meltdown', "Footage emerged today apparently showing Winehouse retrieving drugs from her beehive hairdo and snorting them onstage. The video, posted three days ago on YouTube, was taken during her Zurich performance on October 25."

Amy then played at the Newcastle Academy on November 18 and, for a change, the show got excellent reviews. According to *The Guardian*, she took to the stage and reeled off tracks from *Back To Black*, her voice sounding better than ever, a "roar of jazz and blues". After the bad reviews for the Birmingham show, *The Guardian's* reporter admitted to expecting chaos or worse, being aware that the singer was in the middle of a "torrent of negative interest", but in the end had no choice but to conclude very positively: "The performance is so eerily fantastic that you end up looking for telltale flaws. One song has to be restarted; she is prompted into the segue into 'Bad Thing'; and exposing her bra while taking off a guitar prompts an ongoing obsession with covering her cleavage. But otherwise, this is an absorbing example of a singer living every lyric."

Her next show was at the Empress Ballroom in Blackpool on November 20 and with it, a new scandal broke. Once more, as before, the papers ran with a photograph, the latest in a long line of shocking snaps of the "troubled singer", as she was now frequently referred as. *The Evening Standard* put a picture of Amy on the cover of its Wednesday 21 November edition with the headline: 'Amy Winehouse in new drug riddle'. The related story ran with the headline, 'Is it impolite to ask if you have been to powder your nose, Amy?'. The headline alluded to an adjacent portrait shot of the singer with what *The Evening Standard* called "a suspicious trace of a powdered substance" visible in her right nostril. The photograph was taken as Amy arrived in Blackpool to play the third show of her much-scrutinised UK tour. The *Standard* also made mention of Amy being mentored by Pete Doherty. They quoted Doherty as saying of the predicament she was stuck in: "I speak to Amy almost every day. She just wants her man back for Christmas. They are desperately in love. One good thing is that Blake has got clean since he has been in prison. It's been quite an awakening. Amy stopped doing everything since he went in. She realises how much they have to lose. They are going to lose each other if it carries on." Despite the optimistic tone of Doherty's remarks, the Blackpool photograph suggested he may have been premature. While nobody but Amy knows exactly what the white powder was – and it could have been any number of things – the picture was certainly alarming.

London Lite splashed the same story on its front cover with the headline: 'So just what got up Amy's nose?' Its account of the controversy had more detail. It reported that Amy singled out a young female fan who had a copycat beehive hairstyle and took her backstage. She gave the fan a pair of her earrings and lavished attention on her. But then, *London Lite* offered this comment: "We're not sure if the girl's mum would have been pleased to see her daughter's role model with copious amounts of white powder hanging out of her nose." The paper also reported that Amy signed autographs as Amy Civil.

The Sun covered the story under the headline 'Amy Goes Back to White', a play on *Back To Black*. Its report began by reiterating all the elements of the unfolding drama: "With her husband in prison, mum pleased he's locked up and fans booing her – it seemed things couldn't get any worse for Amy Winehouse. However a new picture emerged today apparently showing the singer with white powder lodged up her nose, suggesting she still has some demons left to battle." While not jumping to any conclusions, especially in light of Pete Doherty's comments the day before that Amy was clean, the report expressed concern at exactly what the white powder in Amy's nose might be.

Meanwhile, over in the US, *Frank* finally saw an American release. It shipped to stores on November 20 and entered the album chart at number 61. It seemed that here at least, Amy could do no wrong. Even her dusted-down debut album was of sufficient interest to earn that respectable chart position, despite the cancellation of her September US tour. Those around Amy must have wondered what the sales would have been like if she *had* made those dates, and driven her voice and charisma deeper into the American public consciousness.

The media picked up on the November 26 issue of *First* magazine (a women's weekly that bills itself as "where smart meet style every week") before it hit news-stands, on account of the magazine carrying an exclusive interview with Amy's mother, Janis. When the magazine actually came out, next to a picture of Amy, the headline exclaimed: 'Thank God Blake's In Prison, says Amy's Mum'. The interview, conducted by Lucy Bulmer, was very candid, offering a fascinating portrait of a mother's mind when her child is in trouble.

Bulmer visited Janis at the London flat she shares with her partner of seven years, Tony. The journalist noted in her article that on the wall hung a double platinum disc for *Back To Black* and, on the mantelpiece, two further awards: a MOJO trophy and an *Elle* magazine Style Award. Bulmer set the scene by neatly summing up the recent catastrophes in Amy's life: "Drink, drugs, bulimia, an impulsive wedding, rows in the street and now her husband has been carted off to prison charged with attempting to pervert the course of justice." She then stepped into the period of time after Blake's incarceration, noting: "According to sources close to the singer, the crisis has left her distraught and leaning even more heavily on heroin." Janis told Bulmer that Amy was not living at the home she and Blake shared in Camden, but was instead staying with an old friend from drama school days.

Janis, who was diagnosed with multiple sclerosis four years earlier, was put in the heart-wrenching position of having to state publicly that her daughter is better off with her husband behind bars: "While they are apart, she will wake up and think, 'What have I done?'" She then goes on to say of her daughter's love for Blake: "If the relationship is meant to be, it will survive this. But Amy's got to love him for him, not because she feels sorry for him or because he's got her doped up."

Another key comment in the interview concerns Amy's use of alcohol. Janis tells Bulmer that Amy first started drinking heavily while a teenager and that on account of getting very nervous about performing, her drinking has spiralled since her career took off. Darcus Beese also makes reference to this in the documentary feature on the DVD *I Told You I Was Trouble – Live In London*. He says Amy takes to the stage certain no one's going to be interested and only walks her way confidently towards magic once she's been touched by the first enthusiasm of the audience. It's a showbiz cliché – insecure, sensitive artist choosing a career that involves standing up on a stage before a crowd to entertain them. Enter the usual coping strategies of the entertainment world – drugs and alcohol. In the world of performing and music, using alcohol as a crutch is nothing out of the ordinary. But what Janis theorises is that the heavy drinking arrived with the live performing – which Amy started to do when she was 18.

Janis then talks about the day Blake was arrested. She says that she and her partner, Tony, were due to head over to Amy and Blake's flat in Camden. Then Amy cancelled, telling her mother by phone, "Don't come to the flat, I'll meet you in a pub." Janis says she thought that was strange. Later the same day, Amy called her again and asked her to pick her up from Hackney. But then, when Janis tried to enact a plan to do that, she couldn't get hold of Amy, who wasn't answering her mobile. Finally, the mystery was cleared up when Alex Winehouse, Amy's brother, called their mother and told her that the police had gone over to Amy and Blake's flat and raided it.

Janis told Bulmer that she did not then get to speak with Amy until the following morning. She called Amy at her friend's house. Amy said to her, "You haven't said anything about Blake," and Janis replied, "That's a bit like saying the sun is out, it must be daytime. I know he's been taken in, what more is there to say?" Bulmer notes at this point that Janis appeared upset, under strain at all the stories about her daughter in the media. What mother wouldn't be? Under constant fear of the phone ringing in the dead of night with terrible news. Under constant scrutiny from the media, everyone wanting to know what she and her ex-husband are going to do? How they're coping? She tells Bulmer that she's heard people talking of Amy going through a belated adolescence and concurs, saying that in her opinion, Amy never had a proper adolescence, with all the predictable tantrums and dramas, crises and catastrophes, because when all her peers were busy being teenagers, Amy was focused entirely on her love of music and the pursuit of a career singing and performing.

At the heart of the interview sits the fact that Janis has never directly broached the subject of drugs with her daughter. She tells Bulmer, "I know, from what people around her have told me, that she has talked about therapy and wanting to come off drugs." She also tells Bulmer that in her opinion, Amy has not been doing drugs for long enough for the abuse to be considered a full blown addiction. She still has hope that Amy will come to her senses. "Most people who are hooked on heroin don't have anything else in their life," she tells Bulmer. "But Amy has her music, her career and a loving family."

Meanwhile, the tour continued. Amy played strong shows at London's Brixton Academy on November 22 and 23 and then turned in an erratic performance at the Hammersmith Apollo on November 24. *NME* reported on the chaos at the Hammersmith show: "Winehouse arrived on stage 45 minutes late, at 22.15, by which time some fans were already demanding refunds for their £30 tickets. Many sections of the crowd were booing before Winehouse took the stage. Midway through the performance Winehouse seemed bored and walked offstage, leaving a backing singer to step forward and take vocal duties. She looked unstable throughout the set and at one point her beehive hair extension nearly fell off. While performing 'Valerie' as part of the show's encore, Winehouse left the stage again, halfway through the song, this time for good, once more leaving a backing singer to fill in until the show ended."

She then headed south to play at the Brighton Centre. Then, a day later, two hours before the doors were set to open for her show at the BIC in Bournemouth on November 27, she cancelled the remainder of the tour. The Brighton date ended up being the last. There were a further eight dates remaining, with the tour scheduled to end on December 17 at London's Brixton Academy. According to *The Times*, the 17-date tour had been calculated to gross £1.25 million. But with the cancellation, the paper reported that Amy was facing bills of up to £500,000.

A spokeperson for Amy told the media: "Amy Winehouse has cancelled all remaining live and promotional appearances for the remainder of the year on the instruction of her doctor. The rigours involved in touring and the intense emotional strain that Amy has been under in recent weeks have taken their toll. In the interests of her health and well-being, Amy has been ordered to take complete rest and deal with her health issues. Refunds for the remaining dates will be issued from the point of purchase."

Amy's statement added: "I can't give it my all onstage without my Blake. I'm so sorry but I don't want to do the shows half-heartedly; I love singing. My husband is everything to me and without him it's just not the same."

Regardless, the machine played on and, on December 10, 'Love Is A Losing Game', the sweetest, most forlorn song on *Back To Black,* was released as a single. Hearing it on the radio was a reminder that this story is about music, should be only about music. It sounded terribly sad, infused with the realities of Amy having cancelled her tour because of Blake being in prison. This was where their love had ended up – the pair of them star-crossed lovers, living on separate sides of a fence.

The award nominations continued streaming in, too. Early in December, news broke of Amy having received no less than six Grammy nominations for *Back To Black*, which had by now sold a staggering 4.5 million copies worldwide. She had been nominated for Album Of the Year, Record Of the Year, Best Female Pop Vocal Performance, Best New Artist, Best Pop Vocal Album and Song Of The Year. The awards ceremony would be held in Los Angeles in February 2008.

After the tour was abandoned, Amy left Camden and moved in with friends in Hackney before she apparently bought a new home in Bow in east London. She was looking for a new start, an opportunity to turn over a new leaf. The photographs kept turning up in the papers – Amy moving out of her Camden flat, Amy going shopping in the dead of night for snacks, Amy coming home in the small hours and, of course, that striking picture of Amy outside in the street, outside the place she was staying, near dawn, wearing just a bra, jeans, barefoot in the freezing November air. That picture spoke volumes, reeked of the tragedy that the Amy Winehouse story had become. Artist, interrupted. Love, interrupted. Music, interrupted. Everyday life, interrupted. Normal life, interrupted.

And so it all seemed to come to an end, a year of living danger-ously. Amy had simply had enough, had her fill; in the words of Martha & the Vandellas, there was nowhere to run, nowhere to hide. She had to take a break from the incessant pace and pressure and seek refuge. The spotlight had become blinding. No more, she seemed to be saying. Leave me alone. The shy north London girl who had stepped into a career of public performance had burned out on the 24-hour-a-day, seven-day-a-week rush of her success. Everybody wanted a piece of her and, in response, she seemed to get smaller and smaller. The brighter the glare of success, the less there was of the 5ft 3in singer. The pounds dropped off her as the pressure mounted. Every escapade and drama and rumour seemed to chip away at her louder-than-life personality. Candid interviews took their toll. Expectations took their toll. And the music started to get shoved into the background. The record sales kept soaring, but the reason why she became world famous was pushed into the background. In its place, Amy Winehouse, the person, the mystery, the great fascination. That guessing game in overdrive – what is wrong with Amy Winehouse?

The year 2007 had seen Amy Winehouse storm the world, break the tricky American market, crack just about every other record-buying territory in the world. It was also a year in which success thrust Amy Winehouse into the role of celebrity. She seemed both comfortable with the attention and acutely uncomfortable with it. She seemed to court attention, yet despise it. As the year went on and *Back To Black* sold and sold and sold, she found herself living like a bug under a microscope. Her every move documented, photographed, analysed, considered, contemplated. Her every utterance held up as a clue to her state of mind. Refreshingly candid remarks about her per-sonal issues in interviews became fuel for the guessing game. The biggest story in the arts in 2007 was this: who is the real Amy Winehouse? What is her life really like? What are her personal issues? What makes her tick? What is she thinking? What kind of lifestyle does she really live? Are any of the rumours true? Is she the victim of gross speculation? Constant exaggeration? Of course, only Amy Winehouse knows the truth. And she's holding what precious few secrets she has left close to her chest. Who knows where she'll go from here? She must know that if the guessing game comes to an end, if rumours are confirmed or denied once and for all, then the media fascination will cease, burst overnight. But for now, the guessing rages on. More clues are dropped. More theories enter the story every day. And Amy continues to live the life of a bug under a microscope, squirming.

Eventually, the music will win out. It has to. Her voice is unique, her songs too vivid, dynamic, classic. Right now, though, as we sit at the end of 2007, things are decidedly out of balance. Her life drowns out the music. It wasn't this way 18 months ago. Then it was all music, music, music. She'll find her way home. All of the chaos and triumph of 2007 will bloom into new songs, new music that channels confusion and sadness and heartbreak into an infectious beat, an unforgettable melody, a confessional lyric that both stings and comforts. Just think how she'll sing those songs. Hair-raising. Until then, we'll think of her barefoot, in her jeans and bra, hair long and flowing, standing there alone, doe-eyed in the blinding headlights, in the dead of a freezing cold November night, a supremely talented artist with no clear direction home.

Epilogue – So Far Away

And then Amy went into rehab on January 24, 2008. *The Guardian* reported on the story the next day, alleging what they believed to have been the trigger for Winehouse to seek help. "The announcement came days after video footage emerged, allegedly showing the troubled 24-year old smoking crack cocaine," the report stated. The news piece then quoted from a statement by her label, Universal Music, "She has come to understand that she requires specialist treatment to continue her ongoing recovery from drug addiction." In reports throughout the media, Universal's statement also mentioned that her admission to rehab had come after talks with "her record label, management, family and doctors." The *Daily Mirror* newspaper reported that Amy had begun treatment at the Capio Nightingale hospital. The specialist facility describes itself on its website as, "Central London's only independent psychiatric hospital providing treatment for drug, alcohol and other addictions and dependencies, eating disorders and other psychiatric issues such as depression, anxiety, stress and trauma." The hospital is located on Lisson Grove, a stone's throw from Marylebone Station.

Amy's admission to rehab immediately cast a question mark over whether or not she would be able to appear and perform at the Grammy awards on February 10. On February 5, she left hospital to visit the US Embassy to seek a visa to attend the Grammy awards. On February 7, news broke that Amy's application for a visa had been declined by the US Embassy. *The Daily Telegraph* quoted from a statement issued by Amy's publicity team, commenting on the news, "Although disappointed with the decision, (Winehouse) has accepted the ruling and will be concentrating on her recovery. Amy has been treated well and fairly by the (US) embassy staff and thanks everyone for their support in trying to make this happen. There will of course be other opportunities and she very much looks forward to visiting America in the near future."

A day later, it was announced that the US Embassy had overturned its initial decision and were now, after all, granting her a visa. Earlier that Friday morning, it had been announced that Amy would appear and perform live by satellite. But despite the u-turn on the visa, Amy stuck with her decision to perform by satellite. A statement from her US publicist explained why: "Unfortunately, due to the logistics involved and timing complications, Amy will not be coming to the US this weekend to perform at the Grammys in Los Angeles."

That Sunday night, Amy swept the Grammy's, picking up five awards: Best New Artist, Best Female Pop Vocal, Song Of The Year, Best Pop Vocal Album and Record Of The Year. Unable to attend or perform at the actual ceremony, on account of the visa issues, she instead participated in the awards ceremony via satellite from Riverside Studios in London. She and her band performed 'You Know I'm No Good' and 'Rehab' – the latter surely a tough song to get through in light of her predicament. The performance of both songs was outstanding and during the evening she received a standing ovation.

When all the glory had died down, she continued her treatment at the Capio Nightingale hospital.

★ ★ ★

By mid February, Amy had left the flat in which she had been living at Bow and moved back to Camden, North London. Her new home was a mews property on a peaceful street. Paparazzi staked out the home and documented the comings and goings of Amy and her inner circle.

On February 20, Amy gave a powerful performance at the Brit Awards in Earl's Court, London. Despite being nominated for Best British Single for her collaboration with Mark Ronson on 'Valerie', Amy didn't take any awards home. She did, however, perform two tracks – a soaring version of 'Valerie' with Ronson and a take of 'Love Is A Losing Game'.

During March and April, Amy was rumoured to have started work on her third album. *NME* reported that the new songs were "very dark" with "many songs themed around the subject of death". It was believed that Amy was scheduled to fly out to the Bahamas to begin work on the much anticipated new album, once more working with producer Salaam Remi. However, the sessions were then cancelled, which meant a new album was unlikely to be released any earlier than 2009.

In the third week of April, Amy received news of three nominations for the Ivor Novello awards, which would be announced at the annual ceremony on May 20. Unusually, she had been nominated twice in the Best Song Musically & Lyrically category – for both 'Love Is A Losing Game' and 'You Know I'm No Good'. The third nomination, in the Best Selling British Song category, saw 'Rehab' receive an inevitable mention.

With the recording of the third album apparently on the back-burner, news emerged that Amy had been collaborating with Mark Ronson on a possible theme song for the next James Bond film, *Quantum Of Solace*. Ronson told the media, "They asked Amy and I think Amy said that if she did it, she'd want to do it with me. So hopefully something will come of it. The demo sounds like a James Bond theme, hopefully. But I don't know if it'll get used."

Then came another headline grabbing crisis. In the early hours of April 23, Amy was apparently involved in a fracas in Camden. *The Daily Mail* offered this account of events, "The award-winning singer is alleged to have butted a passer-by who hailed her a taxi outside a bar in Camden Town, north London, in the early hours of Wednesday after a six-hour pub crawl. The self-confessed junkie is also alleged to have punched Moroccan musician Mustapha el Mounmi in the face because he did not give up a pool table in Bar Tok in Camden. If convicted she could face up to six months in prison and a £2,000 fine."

Two days later, on April 25, she voluntarily attended Holborn Police station, for questioning. Once there, she met with detectives. She was held overnight and then released. *The Daily Telegraph* reported the outcome as follows, "The troubled singer Amy Winehouse has been cautioned for common assault after spending the night in a cell in a central London police station." The formal statement issued by Amy's management, confirmed the detail, "She admitted to a common assault by slapping a man with an open hand and accepted a caution. Amy was fully co-operative with inquiries and apologised for the incident. She thanked the police for their pro-fessional handling of the matter. There will be no further action taken."

To take her mind off the incident, *The Sunday Times* readied to publish its annual list of Britain's richest individuals and announced that Amy had made the list with a personal fortune estimated at £10 million.

On April 27, *The News Of The World* carried an exclusive interview with Mitch Winehouse, under the headline, 'Dad Calls For Amy Winehouse To Be Sectioned'. The report claimed that Mitch believed having Amy sectioned under the Mental Health Act was "the only way to save his daughter from killing herself with drugs." He told them that he was exploring all possible options, "Now is the time to exert whatever pressure we have to try to do it. I've told them she is a danger to herself. There is evidence of self harming and she's a danger to other people because she's attacked someone."

And then as May rolled into action, it was time for Amy to get back to writing new songs for her third album. But getting on smoothly with songwriting was not possible, as Amy found herself in trouble with the authorities.

On May 7, *The Guardian* reported that Scotland Yard had con-firmed arresting a 24-year-old woman. The news story explained that Amy had "been arrested over the possession of drugs in connection with footage handed to police by News International on January 24. The footage, as published in *The Sun* newspaper at the beginning of the year, purported to show Winehouse smoking crack cocaine." Amy was released on bail while the police continued their enquiries.

A week later, on May 14, the matter came to a conclusion, as Amy's spokesman told the media, "Police have confirmed that no action will be taken against Amy Winehouse in relation to an investigation into a video handed to them in January. She was questioned by police last week and released on unconditional bail. They have now concluded their enquiries and no charges will be brought. Amy's bail date to return to Limehouse police station has been cancelled, bringing this matter to an end. Amy is pleased to be able to move on and concentrate on music and particularly looks forward to seeing her fans again at eagerly awaited festival performances this summer."

That out the way, it was time for more awards. On May 22, the 53rd Ivor Novello awards ceremony was held at the Grosvenor Hotel on Park Lane, in London. Amy won the award for Best Song Musically and Lyrically for 'Love Is A Losing Game'. Fashionably late, she arrived at the ceremony just in time to see her father, Mitch, up on stage, collecting the award on her behalf.

Amy then headed off to Portugal to perform at the Rock in Rio Lisboa Festival on May 30. Before a crowd of 90,000, she came onstage late and, according to the BBC, ended up performing only two thirds of her scheduled set list. Her voice was reportedly somewhat hoarse, which affected her delivery. The BBC review said she acknowledged this and, ever wearing her heart on her sleeve, told the crowd, "My voice is not singing right".

She then accepted an invitation to perform privately for Roman Abramovich, the Russian businessman and owner of Chelsea Football Club, and his girlfriend Daria Zhukova. The concert, on June 12, was at the Garage Gallery in Moscow, a new venture by Zhukova, and Amy's performance, for which she was rumoured to have been paid £1 million, was before an elite audience of 300 guests.

Four days later, back in London, Amy was taken ill after fainting at her home. The BBC reported that her father Mitch rushed her to hospital, just to be safe, even though she had recovered from the faint quickly. She then remained at the London Clinic for tests and observation.

On June 22, *The Sunday Mirror* published an interview with Amy's father in which he told them, "She's got emphysema. It's in its early stages, but had it gone on for another month they painted a very vivid picture of her sitting there like an old person with a mask on her face struggling to breathe. With smoking the crack cocaine and the cigarettes her lungs are all gunked up. There are nodules around the chest and dark marks. She's got 70 per cent lung capacity." The interview revealed to the public just how scary Amy's drug abuse had become; the terrible damage already done. *The Mirror* also mentioned that Amy had started on a drug replacement programme – a relief for everybody concerned about her.

Two days later, a spokesperson for Amy played down the alarming scenario her father had created, stating that while "traces" of emphysema had been detected, Amy was not suffering from the fatal lung disease and, with rest and proper medical attention, would be performing as planned at the Nelson Mandela birthday party concert and the Glastonbury Festival, both scheduled at the end of June.

Sure enough, on June 27, Amy overcame all the concerns about her health to appear at the concert in Hyde Park in celebration of Nelson Mandela's 90th birthday. Some reviewers noted that she looked fragile; others that she looked far healthier than she had for some time. After a brief set singing 'Valerie' and 'Rehab' with surprising energy she reappeared at the end of the show for a rendition of the Special AKA hit 'Free Nelson Mandela', alongside Jerry Dammers and the Soweto Gospel Choir. Amy wore a black and white dress and sported a 'Blake' love heart hair clip. She also reportedly changed a line of 'Free Nelson Mandela' to 'Free Blakey, my Fella', a rather ill-judged way of drawing attention to Blake's predicament.

Her performance at Glastonbury on June 29, going on before headliner Jay Z, was less well received. *The Guardian*'s reviewer was not impressed at all: "Her set comprised mainly of the *Back To Black* classics, though none were executed with any lucidity or sense of rhythm. As with the rest of her performance, covers of the Specials' 'A

Message To You Rudy' and 'Hey Little Rich Girl' were almost reduced to instrumentals as she neglected to use her most impressive asset, her voice." Whether it was one of Amy's on or off days didn't change the fact that she appeared visibly happy. *NME* quoted her as telling the crowd, "You don't even know how happy I am to be here tonight. I feel like they should make up a new word in the dictionary for happy and have a picture of me there."

The festival season raging on, Amy appeared at Oxegen in Ireland on July 12 and at T In The Park in Kinross, Scotland, the following day. Here she continued to draw attention to being separated from Blake, this time by dedicating 'Wake Up Alone' to him.

A week later, on July 21, Blake's trial came to its conclusion at Snaresbrook Crown Court in East London. According to *The Daily Telegraph*, "Blake Fielder-Civil, 26, was sentenced to 27 months... Fielder-Civil, of Camden, North London admitted grievous bodily harm and perverting the course of justice for assaulting James King, a pub landlord, and attempting to bribe him £200,000 not to testify last month." The article speculated that Fielder-Civil, who had already served nine months on remand, might be released within a matter of months. The media noted that Amy was not present at the court for the sentencing.

At the end of July, veteran rocker Alice Cooper – another in the long line of rock stars who now repented a misspent youth – sent a public message to Amy via an interview with *The Daily Star*, urging her to turn away from the time honoured cliché of rock'n'roll excess, warning, "I wasn't playing around with things as destructive as they are. Amy's too talented to be messing around like that. At some point she's gotta take a step back and say: Am I gonna live or die? She's got a long career, if she wants it."

On July 28, at around 8:40 pm, the London ambulance services were called to Amy's home in Camden to tend to her after she had been taken ill. She was taken by ambulance to the A&E department at University College hospital. Her spokesman told the press that Amy had suffered from a reaction to medication she was taking and had to be taken to hospital for attention. Doctors kept her in overnight for observation and discharged her the following day.

After a fortnight of rest, Amy performed at the V festival in Staffordshire on August 16, the V festival in Chelmsford on August 17 and then completed her last scheduled live performance for some time on September 6 at Bestival on the Isle of Wight. *The Guardian* panned her Bestival set, which started late, their reviewer saying, "The first song ('Addicted', I think) was barely recognisable, thanks to the fact Amy only sang about 23% of the lyrics. But even when she got her voice back, the whole thing felt a bit nasty, overstepping the increasingly thin line between troubled genius and total shambles. Maybe if we hadn't just spent an hour dancing to Hot Chip, whose rave-tastic set blew the mud halfway to Newport, it wouldn't have seemed so bad. But we had, and in comparison to that, a set of half-sung Sam Cooke and Zutons covers from a woman who could barely stand up straight didn't exactly top off the night in style."

After that, Amy took the break she evidently needed. But then, on October 25, her health failed her again and she was admitted to the London Clinic with a suspected chest infection. The hospital visit sparked more fears that the "traces" of emphesyma found earlier were now taking a stronger hold of the singer's lungs. After various tests and scans, she was discharged on November 2.

Responding to the massive public appetite for Amy's music, on November 24 her label released a box set packaging *Frank* and *Back To Black* together, coupled with outtakes, oddities and demos of the album tracks,

At the end of the month, Amy had another scare and was readmitted to hospital. *The Daily Telegraph* reported her spokesperson as saying that Amy had required medical attention after suffering, "a bad reaction to the combination of medication she has currently been prescribed". Once discharged, some two weeks later Amy flew out of London to clear her head. Her relationship with Blake apparently over, she needed distance to process this and flew to the Caribbean, checking into the Le Sport resort in St Lucia. There she had a chance to reflect. *Now* magazine quoted Amy telling friends at the time, about her marriage, "It's over. There's no way back for us now. It was never going to last. I fancied him like mad, like no one else I've ever known. But it's not enough, is it?"

At the start of 2009, Blake's legal representative filed for divorce. *The Daily Mail* reported that Blake had filed for divorce after seeing photographs of Amy "cavorting with another man in the Caribbean". The other man was 21-year-old Josh Bowman.

The fling with Bowman was not a private affair by this time. Amy had given an interview to *The News Of The World* in which she talked about her new partner. The interview, which ran in January 2009, was candid and lifted the lid on the mystery surrounding her drug addiction. She told the paper that seeing a disturbing drug-addled photograph of herself in a newspaper had kickstarted change and led her to go to St Lucia, "My skin was a spotty mess and I was so pale and skinny. I thought to myself, Girl, you got to sort yourself out or you'll be dead soon. I was depressed, doing drugs and had no life in me at all. Coming here has changed everything." She went on to say that Bowman was making her happy. "He couldn't be more different from my husband, which is not a bad thing. Josh is all handsome and clean and that's what I love about him. I get on like a house on fire with all his family despite them being so posh. When I'm with Josh I don't need drugs to feel good because he makes me feel so amazing."

Amy and Josh met at Le Sport, where he was staying with family. She had originally planned to take a short holiday on the island, but after meeting Josh, she extended her stay.

In an interesting professional move, Amy then announced that she was launching her own record label, Lioness Records. The label's first signing was her 13-year-old goddaughter, Dionne Bromfield. Later in the year, she'd tell *The Sun* that the name was inspired by a lioness pendant that she was given by her grandmother, Cynthia, who had died in the past few years and who she loved dearly: "My nan was like my best friend," she said. "She was the sweetest, strongest, most amazing person I've ever met and when I was thinking of what to call the label I picked up the necklace and knew straight away that I'd call it Lioness, in honour of Cynthia."

The idea that Amy was launching a record label and nurturing the talents of her goddaughter, whose voice she thought was incredible, especially for a 13 year old, seemed to indicate that a more positive outlook was around the corner. But then Josh left the island and Amy was upset, so much so that Mitch flew out to join her.

Still in St Lucia, on February 13, late at night, Amy was rushed to a local hospital, after apparently collapsing. Her spokesman told the media the collapse had occurred after she had run out of her drug replacement medication. It showed how fragile her recovery still was.

Returning to London, Amy looked healthy and tanned. It seemed the worst was behind her but just as the corner was being turned a throwback to the previous September jumped up to upset her balance. Back on September 26 at the Prince's Trust ball, a charity event in London, she sang backing vocals for her goddaughter. Later, a 30-year-old woman named Sherene Flash alleged that she and Amy had an altercation. As a news report on E Online put it, "Accuser Sherene Flash alleges that Winehouse punched her after she approached the singer to take a photograph. Flash was quoted by tabloids shortly after the incident as claiming she had been hit in the eye." Having now filed charges against the singer, Amy voluntarily appeared at a London police station to discuss the incident and assert her innocence. She was then scheduled to appear on March 17 at Westminster Magistrates' Court, where she would enter a plea of not guilty. The charge meant Amy had to cancel an upcoming appearance at the US Coachella festival on April 19.

Having clearly fallen for St Lucia, Amy returned there at the start of April. There were even rumours that she was thinking of buying a property there, so it could become a second home. She was also due to lay down new tracks there with producer Salaam Remi. The brief romance with Josh Bowman was already history – it had reportedly come to an end when he left Le Sport in late January.

Every May there is a jazz festival in St Lucia and that summer Amy decided to make her 'comeback' there but the show, on May 8, proved to be a disaster. *The Daily Telegraph* review was scathing: "She looked nervous and unsure and unsteady on her feet. She hesitated for an uncomfortably long time before taking the microphone; then when she did (for 'Know You Now'), the voice lacked power and conviction. At times she seemed unsure of the words... Half-way through 'Some Unholy War' she called proceedings to a halt declaring, 'Sorry, I'm bored.'" Things got worse – during the set closer, 'Valerie', Amy walked off mid song – to widespread booing – and didn't return. A spokesperson put out a statement following the performance saying the poor weather – the sudden heavy rain – had cut the set short, not Amy.

That same month, Amy had been slated to appear at a special concert at London's Shepherd's Bush Empire to celebrate the 50th anniversary of Island Records. But it was announced on May 22 that she had pulled out. A statement extended an apology to fans who had bought tickets. The cancellation was the latest calamity in the history of Amy's live performances.

In June 2009, Amy's parents Mitch and Janis told ITV News of their fears for Amy's health, saying she was "in denial" about her use of alcohol. Janis said, "The need to rescue her is enormous. Amy is in denial all the time." Her parents said she was still following a drug replacement programme but still drinking and that the drinking was becoming a problem in and of itself. Mitch remarked, "I tried it all – I said, 'Amy you've got to do this, you've got to go to this doctor, you've got to do this, you've got to do that, you're killing me, you're killing your mum'. None of it worked."

The same topic also dominated a documentary called *Saving Amy*, made by Daphne Barak, on location in St Lucia, about Amy and her family's struggle to get clean. Barak would also later publish a book written around the making of the documentary, also called *Saving Amy*.

In July 2009, Amy returned home to London from St Lucia, having been there since April. *The Daily Mail* reported that Amy 'burst into tears' on arriving at Gatwick airport. This aside, she looked physically healthy, wearing a sweater, skirt and white shoes. She had been away, with a brief interlude, for the best part of eight months.

Amy was partly back to deal with the finalizing of her divorce from Blake, which was granted on July 16, and also to attend Westminster Magistrates Court over the incident with Sherene Flash. She appeared in court on July 23, pleading not guilty, and a day later was acquitted of the common assault charge after the judge ruled that he could not be sure the incident was not an accident. Her spokesperson thanked her family, legal team and close friends for their support during the drawn out legal process.

On a positive note, July saw the release of a new album – *Rhythms Del Mundo Classics* – featuring Amy singing a cover of Sam Cooke's 1961 hit 'Cupid'. The song and album, which also featured cover versions by Keane, The Editors, The Killers and The Rolling Stones, was conceived and released as a benefit for Artists Project Earth (APE), a climate change and natural disaster support charity.

On August 22, Amy appeared unannounced at the V festival in Chelmsford, where she first climbed on stage during a set by her equally troubled friend, Babyshambles frontman Pete Doherty. She didn't sing, though, but later in the day she performed with The Specials, singing 'You're Wondering Now' and then contributing backing vocals to 'Ghost Town'.

Performing with a band she respected so much was a welcome distraction from the completion, a week later, of her divorce from Blake, which went through on August 28.

Turning her attention to launching Lioness Records, Amy busied herself with the label's first release on October 12: her goddaughter Dionne Bromfield's debut album. Amy was involved with the production and sang backing vocals on the first single, 'Mama Said'. Amy also sang backing vocals for Dionne when the young singer performed her single on *Strictly Come Dancing*.

The year ended with Amy in more trouble. Having gone to see *Cinderella* staged as a pantomime at the Milton Keynes Theatre in Buckinghamshire, it was reported on December 24 that she ended up "charged with assault after allegedly attacking a theatre manager". The incident came about, as *The Times* explained, when Amy, "entered the pantomime spirit a little too enthusiastically, repeatedly shouting out, 'He's fucking behind you!', during the performance". The theatre's manager, Richard Pound, alleged that Amy "pulled his hair, punched him and kicked him when he asked her to move seats". Amy voluntarily attended Milton Keynes police station on December 23 where she was charged "with a public order offence and common assault following the incident on Saturday night".

At the beginning of 2010, Amy appeared at Milton Keynes Magistrates Court over the incident, pleading guilty to common assault and disorder. According to the BBC, "Winehouse, from

Barnet, north London, was given a two year conditional discharge and must pay £85 in costs. Winehouse... must also pay £100 in compensation to Mr Pound, the theatre's front of house manager."

The same month, Channel 4 aired a new TV documentary called *My Daughter Amy*, which featured Mitch Winehouse's perspective on his daughter's fame and success and the impact her addictions have had on him and the rest of their family.

In May 2010, Amy bought a house in her beloved Camden. *The Evening Standard* later reported that the house, a three storey semi-detached property, cost the singer £1.8 million, and she bought it with a mortgage from private bank, Coutts. She would spend the next 11 months preparing the house, installing a recording studio, and did not move in officially until April 2011.

Meanwhile, Amy and Mark Ronson reunited to record a cover of Leslie Gore's 1963 US number one 'It's My Party' for a Quincy Jones tribute album. It was the first time the pair had worked together since the aborted sessions for the theme to the Bond film *Quantum Of Solace*. The song would surface on the album, *Q Soul Bossa Nostra*, in November.

The reunion continued with Amy returning to live performance on July 6, when she joined Ronson and his band The Business International onstage at London's 100 Club during their debut show. Amy came onstage for half the set, singing only 'Valerie', but it proved ill fated, the BBC reporting that she "forgot many of her words". *NME* claimed she forgot the words to the first verse. Amy later explained that it was a mix-up over which version of 'Valerie' they were performing – and it took her a few bars before she realized Ronson's band were performing the alternate version to the one she had rehearsed.

That summer Amy told *Metro* that her third album would be ready soon and likely out before January 2011. She added that the new album was, "going to be very much the same as my second album, where there's a lot of jukebox stuff and the songs that are... just jukebox, really."

There were also rumours at the time of a collaboration with Roots drummer ?uestlove and Salaam Remi – perhaps the three of them working as a kind of supergroup.

After all the recent turmoil, that summer also saw Amy happily dating film director Reg Traviss. Mutual friends had apparently introduced the couple who lived near one another.

In October 2010, Amy and Fred Perry launched a collaborative fashion line: 17 pieces designed by Amy for Fred Perry. The colours pink and black featured heavily, as did an all prevailing 1950's influence. Amy had long been a fan of the British label. To launch the line, she performed a four-song secret set, accompanied by her keyboard player, at the Fred Perry shop in Spitalfields market. One of the four songs was a jazzy cover of Oasis' 'Don't Look Back In Anger'.

Promoting the collaboration, she told *Glamour UK*, about her battle to conquer her drug addiction. "I'm much healthier now," she said. "I used to use drugs and I haven't used drugs in almost three years. I literally woke up one day and was like, 'I don't want to do this any more.'"

In December, Amy jetted out to Moscow to perform another private concert for another wealthy Russian businessman. As before with Roman Abramovich, she was rumoured to have been paid £1 million. Members of the audience later said the show, Amy's first full show in nearly two years, was outstanding.

The Russian show set Amy back out on the road in earnest. In January 2011 she headed to Brazil to play a five-date mini-tour from January 8–15. There, she was photographed spending time with Rolling Stone Ronnie Wood, who had become a friend. Wood, too, has waged a very public battle with addiction. All five shows in Rio de Janeiro, Florianopolis, Recife and São Paulo, were well received and Amy seemed healthy, radiant, happy, back in control of her talent. Gone were the chaotic shows. It seemed Amy, now 27, had definitively turned a corner.

But, as before, a high was followed by a low. A one-off show in Dubai on February 11 was not well received. The audience booed her performance. A spokesperson said the show was plagued by technical difficulties which had caused Amy's distracted onstage demeanour.

In March, she went into Abbey Road Studios in London with Tony Bennett to record a duet. Mitch, a huge Tony Bennett fan, was ecstatic; Amy too. The track 'Body And Soul' would appear on Tony Bennett's *Duets II* album, out September 2011.

In May, after all the positivity surrounding the Brazil shows, the sad news emerged that Amy had checked herself back into rehab at the Priory Clinic in Roehampton. This new treatment came just ahead of summer commitments to various festival appearances, including a 12-date European tour. Her spokesperson said only that she was admitted on a "doctor's advice". A week later, she checked out, apparently on the understanding that she would continue treatment as an outpatient.

The European tour opened in Belgrade on June 18, a show that was a total disaster. As the BBC put it, "Amy Winehouse has been booed by crowds in Serbia's capital Belgrade after appearing to be too drunk to perform." In footage quickly seen across the web, Amy appeared incoherent, mumbling lyrics, completely out of it. The BBC review continued, focusing on backstage dramas, "The Grammy-award winning singer had been under strict instructions not to drink after recently finishing a course of alcohol rehabilitation in London. Hotel staff on her European tour are said to be under orders to remove alcohol from her room."

After the show, which shocked fans both in the audience and beyond, the next two dates in Istanbul and Athens were cancelled. Then, on June 21, the rest of the tour was cancelled. Her spokesman said she was cancelling the tour to focus on her recovery. "Everyone involved wishes to do everything they can to help her return to her best and she will be given as long as it takes for this to happen." The tour over, Amy went home to her house in Camden.

Tony Bennett, with whom Amy had recorded her duet recently, told *The Guardian* on hearing of Amy's cancelled tour, "Of all the contemporary artists I know, she has the most natural jazz voice, but I'm worried about her and I'm praying for her. She'd help everyone by sobering up and cleaning up her spirituality."

On July 20, she made a surprise guest appearance at the Camden Roundhouse to sing backing vocals for Dionne Bromfield, who was opening for The Wanted. Nobody could have known it would be her last live performance. According to *The Guardian*, reporting on footage of the show, "Winehouse comes on stage and lifts Bromfield up with the force of her embrace. Then, dressed in skinny jeans and a black polo T-shirt she dances sporadically, turning to the drummer, laughing and turning away. When Bromfield briefly holds the microphone to Winehouse's mouth, she does not sing."

On Friday, July 22, Amy saw her mother Janis and also her boyfriend, Reg. Later that evening, she had a routine doctor's appointment at 8:30 p.m. This was in part a way of keeping tabs on her recovery; her father was soon to explain that Amy at this time had been clean of drugs for three years and sober for three weeks.

Confusingly, numerous sources reported Janis Winehouse as having told the *Mirror* that Amy "seemed out of it" when she saw her that Friday. "Out of it" from what, remains unclear. Amy's mother also said how Amy had said goodbye to her, saying, "I love you, Mum."

★ ★ ★

After the doctor's appointment, Amy Winehouse returned to her Camden home and remained there, playing drums deep into the night. At one point her minder told her to keep the noise down as it was getting late. He later recalled that he heard her footsteps as she walked around on the floor above him.

On the morning of Saturday, July 23, the minder checked on Amy and saw she was still sleeping. Not wanting to disturb her, he left her alone. In the afternoon, just before 4pm, the minder checked on Amy again and realized that something was very wrong, that she was not breathing, and called for help. By 3:54pm two ambulances, a paramedic on a bicycle and police had arrived but it was already too late. She was pronounced dead at the scene. At 8:45pm a private ambulance came to the house and five minutes later Amy's body was brought out in a body bag. That evening police sealed off Amy's house, with officers posted outside.

The Metropolitan Police issued a statement, which *The Daily Mail* reported as follows, "Police were called by London Ambulance Service to an address in Camden Square NW1 shortly before 16.05 hrs today, Saturday 23 July, following reports of a woman found deceased. On arrival officers found the body of a 27-year-old female who was pronounced dead at the scene. Enquiries continue into the circumstances of the death. At this early stage it is being treated as unexplained."

At an evening press conference, a spokesperson for the Metropolitan Police said that no cause of death had been identified. The spokesperson was reported by *The Daily Mail* as commenting, "I am aware of reports of a suspected drugs overdose, but I would like to re-emphasize that no post-mortem has yet taken place and it would be inapproporaite to speculate on the cause of death."

Meanwhile, Mitch Winehouse, who was in New York to perform at the Blue Note jazz club, was racing back to London, devastated.

As reports of the singer's death sent shockwaves and sadness across the music industry, fans created a shrine by Amy's house on Camden Square where tributes in all shapes and forms soon built up. Before long the shrine resembled those heaped on the graves of Jim Morrison and Serge Gainsbourg in Paris.

Many news stories cited Amy as having joined the morbid '27 Club', a long list of musicians who had all died prematurely at the age of 27: Kurt Cobain, Brian Jones, Jimi Hendrix, Janis Joplin, Jim Morrison, Robert Johnson.

An autopsy followed on Monday, which proved inconclusive, spelling a two to four week wait for toxicology reports. A short inquest was also opened and adjourned at St Pancras Coroner's Court in London.

That same day, Amy's distraught parents, with Reg Traviss, visited her house and stopped on their way to view the many tributes which included candles, notes, flowers, soft toys and cigarettes.

The family also issued a formal statement to the media, as E Online reported: "Our family has been left bereft by the loss of Amy, a wonderful daughter, sister, niece. She leaves a gaping hole in our lives. We are coming together to remember her and we would appreciate some privacy and space at this terrible time."

A private funeral took place at 12.30pm on Tuesday, July 26. The Jewish ceremony at Edgwarebury Cemetery in North London was attended by 150 friends and family, including Mark Ronson and

Kelly Osbourne. The service, in English and Hebrew, was led by Rabbi Frank Hellner. According to *The Guardian*, a moving eulogy by Mitch Winehouse ended with him saying, "Goodnight, my angel. Sleep tight. Mummy and Daddy love you ever so much." The service closed with a rendition of Carole King's 'So Far Away', Amy's favourite song. Her body was then transferred to the Jewish cemetery in Golder's Green, where during a 20-minute cremation ceremony, *The Sun* reported that Mitch and Janis "wept as they tenderly kissed Amy's coffin". The family, Mitch, Janis and their son Alex, then hosted a two-day shiva at Schindler Hall at Southgate Progressive Synagogue. The evening of the funeral, fans held an impromptu street party outside Amy's house.

As to be expected, rumours started flying about whether songs laid down for her long anticipated third album would be released and at the same time, Amy's back catalogue stormed the global charts, as track and album sales spiralled, driven by grief, intrigue, mystique. Those who knew her and those who were fans, released thousands upon thousands of tributes by blogs, by twitter, by facebook, via interviews.

On July 27, the day after the funeral, Mark Ronson appeared live at the Greenwich Summer Sessions. From the stage, the DJ/producer told the crowd, "It's been a shit week and it's great coming out to play to you guys, that's the great thing about music. If you love Amy and her music make sure you clap your hands right now. I went to her service yesterday and a Rabbi said a person's life is measured in deeds, not years; hers was pretty fucking special. I'm not getting emotional or morbid but it's nice to share this moment with people who appreciate good music. Amy Winehouse was a genius and has made more brilliant music than I'll ever make."

In the end, as Mark Ronson said, what is left is her brilliant legacy. And what a legacy. The voice is with us forever, just as Billie Holiday's is with us forever. And that of countless others before and since. We're also left with the sadness. But her parents say she was happier near the end of her life than she had been in a long time. So there was hope. Who knows what she was thinking as she played drums alone in her house that Friday evening. Who knows what she was thinking when she laid down and her head touched the pillow. Who knows if she suffered or if she went peacefully, blissfully unaware. In her final interview with *The Daily Telegraph*, four months before her death, she spoke of her love of music, yet how hard she found performing, the spotlight and perhaps that quote said everything anyone needs to know about why Amy Winehouse sang, why she needed to sing and why the massive fame that went with her talent was to prove so overwhelming.

"I'm not a natural born performer," she said. "I'm a natural singer, but I'm quite shy, really. You know what it's like? I don't mean to be sentimental or soppy but it's a little bit like being in love, when you can't eat, you're restless, it's like that. But then the minute you go on stage, everything's OK. The minute you start singing."

Discography

You Know I'm No Good
b/w To Know Him Is To Love Him (live) & Monkey Man & You Know I'm No Good (w Ghostface Killah) & You Know I'm No Good (Skeewiff mix)
Released January 2007

Back To Black
b/w Valerie & Hey Little Rich Girl
Released April 2007

Tears Dry On Their Own
b/w You're Wondering Now & Tears Dry On Their Own (Alix Alvarez SOLE Channel Mix) & Tears Dry On Their Own (Al Usher Remix)
Released August 2007

Love Is A Losing Game
b/w Love Is A Losing Game (Kardinal Beats mix)
December 2007

ALBUMS

Frank
Stronger Than Me (Jazz Intro), You Send Me Flying (Cherry), Know You Now, Fuck Me Pumps, I Heard Love Is Blind, Moody's Mood For Love (Teo Licks), (There Is) No Greater Love, In My Bed, Take The Box, October Song, What Is It About Men, Help Yourself, Amy Amy Amy (Outro)
Released October 2003

Back To Black
Rehab, You Know I'm No Good, Me & Mr Jones (Fuckery), Just Friends, Back To Black, Love Is A Losing Game, Tears Dry On Their Own, Wake Up Alone, Some Unholy War, He Can Only Hold Her, Addicted
Released October 2006

Back To Black Deluxe Edition
Rehab, You Know I'm No Good, Me & Mr Jones (Fuckery), Just
Friends, Back To Black, Love Is A Losing Game, Tears Dry On Their
Own, Wake Up Alone, Some Unholy War
He Can Only Hold Her, Addicted,
Bonus Tracks: Valerie, Cupid, Monkey Man, To Know Him Is To Love
Him, Hey Little Rich Girl, You're Wondering Now, Some Unholy
War, Love Is A Losing Game (original demo)
Released November 2007

Frank/Back To Black box set
Released November 2008

APPEARANCES

With Mark Ronson
Valerie
Released October 2007

With Mutya Buena
B Boy Baby
Released December 2007

With Rhythms del Mundo
Cupid
Released July 2009

With Quincy Jones
It's My Party
Released November 2010

With Tony Bennett
Body and Soul
(DUE) Released September 2011

REMIXES

Frank remixes
12″ maxi single
Fuck Me Pumps – Mylo Remix, Fuck Me Pumps – MJ Cole Remix, Stronger Than Me – Harmonic 33 Remix, In My Bed – Bugz In The Attic Vocal Mix, In My Bed – Bugz In The Attic Dub. Take The Box – Seiji's Buggin Mix, Take The Box – Seiji's Buggin Rub
Released July 2007

DVD

I Told You I Was Trouble Live In London
Addicted, Just Friends, Cherry, Back To Black, Wake Up Alone, Tears Dry On Their Own, He Can Only Hold Her, Fuck Me Pumps, Some Unholy War, Love Is A Losing Game, Valerie, Hey Little Rich Girl, Rehab, You Know I'm No Good, Me & Mr Jones, Monkey Man, Outro
Released November 2007